STUDY GUIDE

The Basics of the Christian Life

Sinclair B. Ferguson

LIGONIER MINISTRIES
Renew your Mind.
LIGONIER.ORG | 800-435-4343

421 Ligonier Court, Sanford, FL 32771
Email: info@ligonier.org

Printed in China.

Contents

Introduction

What is a Christian? What does it mean to belong to a church? How can we grow in grace? And how do we live the Christian life to the very end? How we answer these questions has a huge impact on the course of our Christian lives. In this series, Dr. Sinclair B. Ferguson carefully explains the basics of the Christian life and helps us know what it means to be a Christian and how to live abundantly to the glory of God.

This study guide is a companion to the video teaching series. Whether you are using the DVDs, streaming the videos on Ligonier.org, or going through the course in Ligonier Connect, this resource is designed to help you make the most of the learning experience. For each message in the series, there is a corresponding lesson in this guide. Here is what you will find in each lesson:

INTRODUCTION	The introduction is a brief paragraph that summarizes the content covered in the lecture and considered in the study guide lesson. **How to use:** Use the introduction to each lesson to get a sense of the big picture before watching the video. Refer to these statements as you work through the study guide to remind you of what you have already covered and where you are headed.
LEARNING GOALS	The learning goals are the knowledge and skills the study guide lesson will endeavor to equip you with as you work through the lecture content. **How to use:** Familiarize yourself with the goals of each lesson before engaging with its contents. Keeping the overall purpose in mind as you watch each video and reflect on or discuss the questions will help you get the most out of each lesson.
KEY IDEAS	The key ideas are the major points or takeaways from the lecture. **How to use:** Use these ideas to prepare yourself for each lesson and to review previous lessons. They describe specifically the knowledge each lecture is communicating.

REFLECTION & DISCUSSION QUESTIONS	The questions are the guided reflection and/or discussion component of the lesson that are intended to help you prepare for, process, and organize what you are learning. **How to use:** Reflect on individually or discuss in a group the questions in the order in which they appear in the lesson. The timestamps in the right margin indicate where the answers to questions during the video can be found.
PRAYER	The prayer section offers suggestions for how to close the lesson in prayer with respect to what was taught in the lecture. **How to use:** Consider using each lesson's prayer section as a guide to personal or group prayer. These sections follow the ACTS prayer model, which you can learn more about in R.C. Sproul's Crucial Questions booklet *Does Prayer Change Things?* This helpful guide is available as a free e-book at Ligonier.org.
REVIEW QUIZ	The review quiz is a set of six multiple-choice questions that appears at the end of each lesson. **How to use:** Use each quiz to check your comprehension and memory of the major points covered in each lecture. It will be most beneficial to your learning if you take a lesson's quiz either sometime between lessons or just before you begin the next lesson in the study guide.
ANSWER KEY	The answer key provides explanations for the reflection and discussion questions and answers to the multiple-choice questions in the review quiz. **How to use:** Use the answer key to check your own answers or when you do not know the answer. Note: Do not give in too quickly; struggling for a few moments to recall an answer reinforces it in your mind.

Study Schedules

The following table suggests four plans for working through *The Basics of the Christian Life* video teaching series and this companion study guide. Whether you are going through this series on your own or with a group, these schedules should help you plan your study path.

	Extended 14-Week Plan	Standard 12-Week Plan	Abbreviated 6-Week Plan	Intensive 4-Week Plan
Week	**Lesson**			
1	*	1	1	1–3
2	1	2	2 & 3	4–6
3	2	3	4 & 5	7–9
4	3	4	6 & 7	10–12
5	4	5	8 & 9	
6	5	6	10 & 11	
7	6	7	12	
8	7	8		
9	8	9		
10	9	10		
11	10	11		
12	11	12		
13	12			
14	*			

* For these weeks, rather than completing lessons, spend your time discussing and praying about your learning goals for the study (the first week) and the most valuable takeaways from the study (the last week).

1

Becoming a Christian

INTRODUCTION

Every believer can benefit from thoughtfully considering the basics of the Christian life. One of the most basic questions we should ask ourselves is, What does it mean to be a Christian? Sometimes, answering a question like this requires us to know what a Christian is not. In this lesson, Dr. Ferguson draws from John 8 to provide an overview of the spiritual condition and characteristics of the unbeliever so that we can ask if we are walking in the darkness or in the light.

LEARNING GOALS

When you have finished this lesson, you should be able to:

- Recognize the benefits of reviewing the basics of Christianity for ongoing spiritual growth
- Understand the historical and cultural context of Jesus' teaching in John 8
- List the three defining characteristics of the unbeliever

KEY IDEAS

- Every Christian should regularly revisit the basic principles of Christianity.
- All who are separated from Christ dwell in spiritual darkness, no matter how religious they may appear.
- Christ alone is the only means of salvation for sinners.

REFLECTION & DISCUSSION QUESTIONS

Before the Video

What Do You Think?

Take a moment to answer the following questions. They will prepare you for the lecture.

- Why are you undertaking this study about the basics of the Christian life? What do you hope to gain from it?

- Do you think that mature Christians should bother with reviewing the basics of the faith? Why or why not?

Scripture Reading

Again Jesus spoke to them, saying, "I am the light of the world. Whoever follows me will not walk in darkness, but will have the light of life."

—John 8:12

- According to this passage, what is the proof that a person has the light of life and is not walking in darkness?

During the Video

Answer the following questions while you watch the video. They will guide you through the lecture.

The Background of Jesus' Teaching *0:00–12:30*

- Where did the Jews live during the Feast of Booths and why?

- What were the two elements of symbolism on display during the Feast of Booths?

The Response to Jesus' Teaching *12:30–23:17*

- How did the Jews respond when Jesus said that He could set them free?

- When the Jews claimed that God was their Father, how did Jesus reply and provide for us a way of knowing if God is our Father?

After the Video

Answer the following questions after you have finished the lecture. They will help you identify and summarize the major points.

- How were the symbols of water and light during the Feast of Booths supposed to serve as reminders to the Jews?

  If you are in a group, have the members discuss the ways in which recalling God's saving acts in the exodus could have been beneficial to the Jews as they celebrated the Feast of Booths. For practical application, consider discussing the following: How can recalling God's past works—both in the world and in our own lives—strengthen our faith, courage, and hope in our current circumstances? Be specific.

- What are the three characteristics of unbelievers, as seen in Jesus' teaching in John 8?

  If you are in a group, have the members discuss whether they think that unsaved people view themselves in these ways. Consider asking group members to recall their own conversions. Did they see themselves in the way Jesus described? Why or why not?

- According to John 8:43–44, who does Jesus identify as the true father of His hearers? Why was that the case?

  If you are in a group, have the members discuss the following: Is there any such thing as spiritual neutrality, or is every person either a son of God or a son of Satan? Are very moral and religious unsaved people in a neutral category? Why or why not?

PRAYER

Commit what you have learned from God's Word in this lesson to prayer.

- Praise God that He has provided the way of salvation through Jesus Christ.
- Confess ways in which you choose darkness over light in your daily actions, speech, and attitudes.
- Thank God for transferring you from the kingdom of darkness to the kingdom of light.
- Ask God to grant you fresh insight and opportunities for spiritual growth as you consider the basics of the Christian life.

REVIEW QUIZ

Use these multiple-choice questions to measure what you learned from this lesson.

1. What was significant about the final day of the Feast of Booths?
    a. No water was drawn.
    b. The lights were not lit.
    c. Water was drawn, and the lights were lit.
    d. Water was not drawn, and the lights were not lit.

2. What truth does Jesus communicate to the Jews in John 8:12–20?
    a. They are failing to obey the Ten Commandments.
    b. They are engaging in idolatry.
    c. They are walking in spiritual darkness.
    d. They are neglecting the widow and orphan.

3. What aspect of the Jews' condition does Jesus address in John 8:21–30?
    a. Moral failure
    b. Roman oppression
    c. Corrupt religious leaders
    d. Spiritual deadness

4. What does Jesus tell Nicodemus in John 3:3 regarding the requirement for entering the kingdom of God?
    a. He must sell his belongings.
    b. He must repent of his sin.
    c. He must obey God's law.
    d. He must be born again.

5. The Jews assumed that they were spiritually alive.
    a. True
    b. False

6. When Jesus tells the Jews that they are slaves to sin, whose sons do they claim to be?
    a. Abraham's
    b. Isaac's
    c. Jacob's
    d. Joseph's

Answer Key—Becoming a Christian

REFLECTION & DISCUSSION QUESTIONS

Before the Video

What Do You Think?

These are personal questions. The answers should be based on your own knowledge and experience.

Scripture Reading

- According to this passage, what is the proof that a person has the light of life and is not walking in darkness?

  The proof that one has the light of life, according to John 8:12, is that he follows Jesus Christ. Jesus spoke these words during the Feast of Booths, and in these words, Jesus was telling the people what it meant to become and to be a Christian.

During the Video

The Background of Jesus' Teaching

- Where did the Jews live during the Feast of Booths and why?

  During this time, the Jews gathered in Jerusalem and lived in makeshift tents. Living in these tents served as a reminder of how God had brought His people out of bondage in Egypt, as Israel had lived in tents while they wandered in the wilderness for forty years on the way to the promised land.

- What were the two elements of symbolism on display during the Feast of Booths?

  The use of water and light served as symbols during the feast. Water and light were both significant aspects of the Israelites' experience during the exodus as they traveled through the desert from Egypt to the promised land.

The Response to Jesus' Teaching

- How did the Jews respond when Jesus said that He could set them free?

  The Jews replied that they had never been in bondage to anyone (John 8:33). According to Dr. Ferguson, this was a typical and distinctively Jewish response. Their response to Jesus indicated that they were, in fact, in spiritual bondage.

- When the Jews claimed that God was their Father, how did Jesus reply and provide for us a way of knowing if God is our Father?

  Only those who love the Son truly have God as their Father, because the Father Himself sent the Son to earth. Jesus replied to them, "If God were your Father, you would love me, for I came from God and I am here" (John 8:42). One cannot have the Father without also embracing the Son.

After the Video

- How were the symbols of water and light during the Feast of Booths supposed to serve as reminders to the Jews?

  The water was a reminder of how God had given them water in the desert, and the lights were a reminder of how God had led them by the pillar of cloud by day and the pillar of fire by night during their forty years in the desert.

- What are the three characteristics of unbelievers, as seen in Jesus' teaching in John 8?

  Unbelievers walk in spiritual darkness, live in spiritual death, and are held in spiritual bondage. Jesus discusses spiritual darkness in John 8:12–20, spiritual death in John 8:21–30, and spiritual bondage in John 8:31–36.

- According to John 8:43–44, who does Jesus identify as the true father of His hearers? Why was that the case?

  In this passage, Jesus says, "You are of your father the devil, and your will is to do your father's desires." All who are not children of God are children of the devil. There is no neutral category, even for those unbelievers who are highly moral and do good works for others. Only those who listen to Jesus' words and believe His words to be the truth are children of God.

REVIEW QUIZ

Lesson 1

1. **D.**
   During the final day of the Feast of Booths, neither water nor lights were included in the celebration. This fact makes Jesus' invitation to come to Him and drink, as well as His claim to be the Light of the World, even more dramatic when compared to the absence of water and light on the final feast day.

2. **C.**
   In John 8:12–20, Jesus tells the Jews that apart from Him, they are walking in spiritual darkness. These words would have been especially impactful since they were spoken on the last day of the Feast of Booths. On this day, none of the brilliant feast lights were lit, and the contrast between this darkness and the previous light would have been obvious.

3. **D.**
   Jesus makes clear that the Jews are spiritually dead, and unless they believe in Him, they cannot be saved, as He says, "Unless you believe that I am he you will die in your sins" (John 8:24).

4. **D.**
   Jesus told Nicodemus that he had to be born again in order to see the kingdom of God. In saying this, Jesus indicated that the natural condition of man means that he walks in spiritual darkness and is unable to see and understand the gospel.

5. **A.**
   The Jews assumed that God was their Father despite the fact that they were rejecting the Son who had been sent by the Father. They appealed to their physical heritage and status as God's chosen nation, but spiritually, God was not their true Father.

6. **A.**
   The Jews claimed to have Abraham as their father, but Jesus pointed out the contradiction in John 8:39–40 that they did not do the works that Abraham did, thus revealing they were not Abraham's children from a spiritual standpoint.

2

Being a Christian

INTRODUCTION

What does it mean to be a Christian? While every believer might answer this question somewhat differently, Scripture gives us an overarching framework for understanding who we have become as a result of the redemptive work of Christ. In this lesson, Dr. Ferguson explores the two fundamental identities that mark Christians, as well as the significance of these identities for the Christian life.

LEARNING GOALS

When you have finished this lesson, you should be able to:

- Understand what it fundamentally means to be a Christian
- Describe the two major pictures that express the Christian's identity

KEY IDEAS

- It is impossible for man to rightly know his true identity apart from the Bible.
- Believers receive a new identity in relation to the Father, the Son, and the Holy Spirit.
- Healthy Christian growth requires understanding and living in light of our identity in Christ.

REFLECTION & DISCUSSION QUESTIONS

Before the Video

What Do You Think?

Take a moment to answer the following questions. They will prepare you for the lecture.

- How would you describe yourself as a Christian in one sentence?

- How does the identity of a believer differ from that of an unbeliever?

Scripture Reading

> *For all who are led by the Spirit are sons of God. For you did not receive the spirit of slavery to fall back into fear, but you have received the Spirit of adoption as sons, by whom we cry, "Abba! Father!" The Spirit himself bears witness with our spirit that we are children of God.*
>
> —Romans 8:14–16

- According to this passage, what has the Christian received from God? What is the Christian's response to receiving this gift?

During the Video

Answer the following questions while you watch the video. They will guide you through the lecture.

The First Aspect of Our Identity *0:00–18:04*

- What is the first primary identity of the Christian?

- What are the two dimensions in which this identity is established?

The Second Aspect of Our Identity *18:04–23:41*

- What is the second primary identity of the Christian?

- Why didn't Jesus experience conflict or tension between His identity as God's Son and His identity as God's Servant?

After the Video

Answer the following questions after you have finished the lecture. They will help you identify and summarize the major points.

- When Adam and Eve sinned in the garden, how did that affect their identity as God's children?

If you are in a group, have the members discuss how the fatherhood of God affects their lives on a day-to-day basis. How does this truth strengthen and enable them, and if they struggle with viewing God as Father, why is that the case?

- Read Romans 8:15–23. What are the benefits of being children of God? What thing must we experience in this life before we are glorified?

If you are in a group, have the members discuss the following questions: If God is a loving Father, why would He require and allow His children to suffer in this life? Is this a contradiction in His character? Why or why not?

- Do you find it more difficult to live out your identity as God's child or your identity as Christ's servant? Why do you think this is the case, and how can the teaching in this lesson and the associated Scripture passages help you grow in this area?

If you are in a group, have the members discuss their answers to the above questions.

PRAYER

Commit what you have learned from God's Word in this lesson to prayer.

- Praise God for His loving character to become a Father to the wayward and lost.
- Confess areas of your life where you neglect your identity as a servant of Christ.
- Thank God for the Holy Spirit's witness to you of your identity as a child of God.
- Ask God to give you greater understanding of your identity as a child and as a servant for greater joy and obedience in your Christian life.

REVIEW QUIZ

Use these multiple-choice questions to measure what you learned from this lesson.

1. What did Dr. Ferguson name as one of the great crises in the Western world today?
   a. The crisis of immorality
   b. The crisis of inefficiency
   c. The crisis of inequality
   d. The crisis of identity

2. Which book of the Bible contains the Servant Songs of Christ?
   a. Genesis
   b. Isaiah
   c. Psalms
   d. Matthew

3. Which of the following terms explains why some people find it difficult to view God as a Father because of their experience with their earthly fathers?
    a. Realism
    b. Reactionism
    c. Projectionism
    d. Confirmationism
4. Which of the following titles does the religious-yet-unconverted person *not* instinctively use to call out to God?
    a. Master
    b. Father
    c. Lord
    d. Creator
5. The Apostle Paul compares our spiritual adoption to the Jewish customs of adoption in his day.
    a. True
    b. False
6. Which of the following is the Christian *not* set free from?
    a. Sin's dominion
    b. Slavery to self
    c. Service to God
    d. Self-obsession

Answer Key—Being a Christian

REFLECTION & DISCUSSION QUESTIONS

Before the Video

What Do You Think?

These are personal questions. The answers should be based on your own knowledge and experience.

Scripture Reading

- According to this passage, what has the Christian received from God? What is the Christian's response to receiving this gift?

  The Christian has received the Spirit of adoption. When a person is saved, he goes from being God's enemy to being God's beloved child. This gift of adoption enables a believer to call out to God as Father from the heart. While we may go through periods of doubt or questioning, the Spirit is always at work to remind us of who we are as children of God.

During the Video

The First Aspect of Our Identity

- What is the first primary identity of the Christian?

  The first primary identity of the Christian is as a child of God. Christians are children of God with all the privileges and benefits of sonship. While some people may believe that every person is a child of God, the truth is that as a result of the fall, only believers are true children of God (John 1:12–13). God is the Creator of all people, but He is Father only of the redeemed.

- What are the two dimensions in which this identity is established?

  First, a new relationship or status needs to be established with God. This relationship is spoken of in the New Testament in terms of God's adopting us into His family when we had previously been spiritual orphans. In Christ, not only are we declared righteous, but we are also brought into the family of God. The second dimension is that we receive a new instinct toward God. Through the regenerating work of the Holy Spirit, we are able to cry out, "Abba, Father," and know that we are cared for and loved by God.

The Second Aspect of Our Identity

- What is the second primary identity of the Christian?

  In addition to being a child of God, the Christian is also a servant of Christ. During His life and earthly ministry, Jesus viewed Himself as a servant, waking every day to listen to His Father's voice and to do His will. He willingly yielded to the Father in all things, and as Christians we are to serve Christ as Lord in same manner in which He served the Father.

- Why didn't Jesus experience conflict or tension between His identity as God's Son and His identity as God's Servant?

  Jesus did not experience conflict between these two identities because He was a Son who loved His Father and lived to please and obey Him in all things. These two identities are not fundamentally in conflict with one another; Adam and Eve were originally created to be children of God who would perfectly obey Him as evidence of their relationship.

After the Video

- When Adam and Eve sinned in the garden, how did that affect their identity as God's children?

  As a result of their sin, Adam and Eve became spiritual orphans and were no longer able to think about God as their loving heavenly Father until God Himself restored that relationship. In the gospel, we see God's heart to bring spiritual orphans into His family so that they might call Him "Abba, Father."

- Read Romans 8:15–23. What are the benefits of being children of God? What must we experience before we are glorified?

  According to Romans 8:15–23, the children of God are freed from slavery and fear, have received the Holy Spirit, are heirs of God and fellow heirs with Christ, will be glorified, and will receive redeemed bodies. Yet according to Romans 8:17, we must first suffer with Him before we are glorified with Him.

- Do you find it more difficult to live out your identity as God's child or your identity as Christ's servant? Why do you think this is the case, and how can the teaching in this lesson and the associated Scripture passages help you grow in this area?

  These are personal application questions. Answers will vary but should take into consideration the main themes of this lesson.

REVIEW QUIZ

Lesson 2

1. **D.**
   According to Dr. Ferguson, one of the great crises in the Western world today is the crisis of identity. This crisis stems from a cultural rejection of the revelation of God in Scripture, causing people to wonder, "Who am I?" With the embrace of secular humanism, man has lost his ability to understand his true identity.

2. **B.**
   The Servant Songs are found in the book of Isaiah. For further study, see Isaiah 42, 49, 50, and 52–53, which picture Jesus as the Servant of the Lord.

3. **C.**
   Some people struggle with the concept of God as a Father because of their negative experiences with their earthly fathers. This is known as the error of projectionism, in which a person takes his personal experience of an earthly father and attributes those same qualities to God. The antidote to distorted views of fatherhood is to study what Scripture has to say about God as a perfect Father.

4. **B.**
   The religious-yet-unconverted person does not instinctively call out to God as Father because he does not possess the Holy Spirit, who enables us to call out to God in this manner. The unconverted person may cry out to God in general, but rarely will he view God as a Father.

5. **B.**
   The Apostle Paul uses the analogy of adoption in light of Roman law and Roman practices of adoption. In Roman society, those who were adopted would receive provision and resources from their new family, and their new father would care for them.

6. **C.**
   Through faith in Christ, we are set free from the dominion of sin, bondage to self, and obsession with self. However, the Christian is never free from service to God. In fact, part of the freedom the Christian enjoys is the freedom to serve God rather than sin and self.

3

Belonging to the Church

INTRODUCTION

Western culture glorifies individualism, such that the concept of belonging to and functioning in a community context, in many ways, has been lost. Is Christianity compatible with the idea of individualism? In this lesson, Dr. Ferguson shows from Scripture that Christ's purpose is to build a community of worshipers who belong not only to Him but also to one another.

LEARNING GOALS

When you have finished this lesson, you should be able to:

- Recognize the importance of the local church in the life of the Christian
- Understand Jesus' driving mission to build His church as a unified body
- List and explain the five characteristics of a Spirit-filled church

KEY IDEAS

- The church was at the very heart of Jesus' plan for His ministry.
- The Christian life is not individual, but corporate.
- Scripture provides us with a clear picture of a faithful and well-functioning church.

REFLECTION & DISCUSSION QUESTIONS

Before the Video

What Do You Think?

Take a moment to answer the following questions. They will prepare you for the lecture.

- Is it necessary to belong to a local church to be a faithful Christian? Why or why not?

- What would you list as the fundamental components of a biblical church?

Scripture Reading

Now when Jesus came into the district of Caesarea Philippi, he asked his disciples, "Who do people say that the Son of Man is?" And they said, "Some say John the Baptist, others say Elijah, and others Jeremiah or one of the prophets." He said to them, "But who do you say that I am?" Simon Peter replied, "You are the Christ, the Son of the living God." And Jesus answered him, "Blessed are you, Simon Bar-Jonah! For flesh and blood has not revealed this to you, but my Father who is in heaven. And I tell you, you are Peter, and on this rock I will build my church, and the gates of hell shall not prevail against it.

—Matthew 16:14–18

- What comfort does this verse contain for those who belong to Christ and His church?

During the Video

Answer the following questions while you watch the video. They will guide you through the lecture.

The Beginnings of the Church *0:00–12:04*

- Why is Jesus' statement in Matthew 16:18 significant?
- What is significant about the pronouns used in the Lord's Prayer?

The Blueprint for the Church *12:04–24:22*

- What element of a Spirit-filled church has almost disappeared in the Christian church today?
- In what ways was the church in Acts a sharing community?

After the Video

Answer the following questions after you have finished the lecture. They will help you identify and summarize the major points.

- Why did Jesus not speak about the church regularly to His disciples during His earthly ministry?

  If you are in a group, have the members discuss the following: Does the rest of the New Testament place an emphasis on the church? Where and how is this seen in Scripture?

- According to Dr. Ferguson, why might the testimony of the church as a whole be a more powerful witness to unbelievers than individual testimonies?

  If you are in a group, have the members compare and contrast the ways in which an individual's testimony and a church's witness can affect unbelievers and serve as an evangelistic tool.

- What does it mean that the early church was a "multicultural community"?

  If you are in a group, have the members discuss what evidence of this multiculturalism they see on display in their churches. Also, have members discuss whether they intentionally seek to cultivate relationships in the church with brothers and sisters who are different from them, as well as ways they might seek to grow in this area.

PRAYER

Commit what you have learned from God's Word in this lesson to prayer.

- Praise God for Christ's work in bringing His people together in one body.
- Confess any times when you have neglected or doubted the importance of the church.
- Thank God that He has united you to the church in Christ through the Holy Spirit.
- Ask God to show you how to best use your spiritual gifts to serve your local church.

REVIEW QUIZ

Use these multiple-choice questions to measure what you learned from this lesson.

1. As noted in this lecture, to which of the following has Christ called us?
   a. Creation
   b. Culture
   c. Character
   d. Community

2. Which of the following is *not* included in the concept of being a sharing community?
    a. Sharing our lives with each other
    b. Forsaking our claims to personal property
    c. Sharing our possessions and giving to those who have needs
    d. Realizing that our individual families are part of a greater spiritual family
3. What aspect of the church does the practice of praying together fall under?
    a. A learning community
    b. A sharing community
    c. A worshiping community
    d. A multicultural community
4. Paradoxically, the church in Acts 2 was so different from the world that people didn't want to join it, yet people were crowding into the church to be saved.
    a. True
    b. False
5. Many of the New Testament pictures of Christianity are individual rather than communal.
    a. True
    b. False
6. According to the lecture, which element of the church can serve to draw people into deeper relationships with one another?
    a. Praying together
    b. Attending Bible study together
    c. Taking the Lord's Supper together
    d. Serving others together

Answer Key—Belonging to the Church

REFLECTION & DISCUSSION QUESTIONS

Before the Video

What Do You Think?

These are personal questions. The answers should be based on your own knowledge and experience.

Scripture Reading

- What comfort does this verse contain for those who belong to Christ and His church?

  In this verse, Jesus promises that Satan will not prevail against His church. Though the church is the target of Satan's schemes and faces the hostility of the world, the church can never be destroyed because God has promised to sustain it.

During the Video

The Beginnings of the Church

- Why is Jesus' statement in Matthew 16:18 significant?

  This statement comes at a decisive point in Jesus' ministry, and it also comes at a turning point in the gospel of Matthew. From this point onward, Jesus begins to explain to His disciples what it means that He is the Christ and how He will build the church as the One who came to die for sins and to rise again as our Lord and Savior. The statement also contains the central point of the gospel of Matthew. Here, Jesus makes clear that He has come into the world not just to save individuals but to build a community of believers.

- What is significant about the pronouns used in the Lord's Prayer?

  The prayer uses the plural pronouns our *and* us, *as opposed to the singular pronouns* my *and* me. *The Lord's Prayer teaches us that we never exist as isolated Christians; we have been brought into the fellowship of Jesus Christ to belong to one another.*

The Blueprint for the Church

- What element of a Spirit-filled church has almost disappeared in the Christian church today?

  Many churches today are not learning communities. The emphasis is often on what we think we need to do rather than on what God does to us and in us through His Word. As a result of this mind-set, the Word is infrequently expounded to the degree that it ought to be.

- In what ways was the church in Acts a sharing community?

  They shared their lives and their possessions, loved and cared for one another, used their gifts to serve one another, and understood that their physical families were part of a larger spiritual family. This sharing community was a practical expression of how the gospel should affect daily living.

After the Video

- Why did Jesus not speak about the church regularly to His disciples during His earthly ministry?

  Jesus understood that His disciples had almost no idea what the church would look like because they had very little idea of the kind of Messiah He was. Rather than speaking about the church directly, Jesus instead gave His disciples various pictures to indicate that, while He had come into the world to save individual sinners, His goal was to bring them together to create a new community of God's people.

- According to Dr. Ferguson, why might the testimony of the church as a whole be a more powerful witness to unbelievers than individual testimonies?

  In a postmodern culture, people tend to say, "If that works for you, then that's fine." The testimony of an isolated individual is simply interpreted as each person doing what works best for him. But when people witness the entire church together, they realize that nothing else can parallel the uniqueness of this type of community. While they may even hate what the church stands for, they are often attracted to the outworking of the gospel that creates such a community.

- What does it mean that the early church was a "multicultural community"?

  As a multicultural community, the church included both Jews and gentiles, masters and slaves, rich and poor, men and women, single and married, young and old. When God creates a new community in Jesus Christ, that new community will always have some type of diversity. This diversity in the church can serve as a powerful witness to the world because of the various people being brought together for the sake of the gospel.

REVIEW QUIZ

Lesson 3

1. **D.**
   Christ has called us not only to Himself as individuals, but to one another as a community. As Christians, we have been brought into the fellowship of Jesus Christ to belong to one another as brothers and sisters in the family of God.

2. **B.**
   The church in Acts was generous and sacrificial in giving their personal possessions to help others. They did not, however, embrace the ideals of communism or abandon the idea and legitimacy of owning personal property.

3. **C.**
A worshiping community is one that prays together. Dr. Ferguson notes that in worship and prayer, we become what God has intended us to be. As the church prays together, not only does it worship God together, but it also is able to better practice the "one anothers" of Scripture because its members are connected to one another.

4. **A.**
Dr. Ferguson noted that, paradoxically, people hesitated to join the church in Acts 2 because it was so different from the world, yet at the same time, they were drawn to it because it was so different from the world. By being distinct from the world, the church was able to show people what they were missing apart from Christ.

5. **B.**
The New Testament most often pictures Christianity in terms of the community rather than as isolated individuals. Jesus is the Good Shepherd, and as the Shepherd gathers in His sheep to Himself, this also brings His sheep closer to each other. When we are called to faith in Jesus Christ, we're called not only to come to Him but also to come nearer to each other.

6. **A.**
These answers are not mutually exclusive, but prayer was particularly emphasized in this lecture for its ability to bring people closer together. Though prayers are directed to God, people who pray together can hear the hearts of their fellow believers, the concerns of others, and the needs of the fellowship. In these ways, they can be drawn into deeper relationships with each other.

4

Means of Grace: God's Word

INTRODUCTION

All Christians ought to have a desire to grow in their faith. But how does this growth occur? What resources has God provided to enable us to accomplish this goal? In this lecture, Dr. Ferguson explores one of the means that God uses to bring us to spiritual maturity: His Word. Through God's Word, believers are equipped to faithfully live the Christian life.

LEARNING GOALS

When you have finished this lesson, you should be able to:

- Recognize how the Bible is a God-given instrument for our spiritual growth
- List and explain the three reasons why Scripture is important
- Identify the four ways in which the Bible is profitable for believers

KEY IDEAS

- God has provided specific means through which we are able to grow spiritually, which are commonly referred to as the means of grace.
- The Word of God is absolutely central to living the Christian life.
- The Bible itself does not save, but it reveals to us the One who is able to save.

REFLECTION & DISCUSSION QUESTIONS

Before the Video

What Do You Think?

Take a moment to answer the following questions. They will prepare you for the lecture.

- If a new believer asked you for advice on how to grow spiritually, what would you say?

- Is it possible to experience spiritual growth apart from the Bible? Explain why or why not.

Scripture Reading

> *But as for you, continue in what you have learned and have firmly believed, knowing from whom you learned it and how from childhood you have been acquainted with the sacred writings, which are able to make you wise for salvation through faith in Christ Jesus. All Scripture is breathed out by God and profitable for teaching, for reproof, for correction, and for training in righteousness, that the man of God may be competent, equipped for every good work.*
>
> —2 Timothy 3:14–17

- What is Scripture able to do? In what four ways is the Word of God profitable for believers?

During the Video

Answer the following questions while you watch the video. They will guide you through the lecture.

Powerful to Save *0:00–17:30*

- What is the first reason why it is important to study Scripture and belong to a church where Scripture is faithfully expounded?

- How do people often discover the truth of Scripture?

- What is the second reason why studying Scripture is important for Christians?

Powerful to Sanctify *17:30–26:29*

- What did George Whitefield do as an expression of the proper disposition of the Christian toward the Word of God?

- What was called "the crying need in our generation"?

- What is the third reason why Christians should study the Bible?

After the Video

Answer the following questions after you have finished the lecture. They will help you identify and summarize the major points.

- What does it mean that the Bible is God-breathed?

  If you are in a group, have the members discuss the following: Should we expect God to communicate to us outside of His Word? Why or why not? If so, in what ways?

- How does the story of Jacob's wrestling with the angel of the Lord serve as a picture of the impact that Scripture makes on our lives?

  If you are in a group, discuss the following: How has the Word of God humbled you as it did Jacob? Give specific and concrete examples.

- How would you respond to someone who says that we need traditions apart from the Bible to faithfully live the Christian life?

  If you are in a group, discuss the following: Is tradition inherently bad? What are some examples of the church's faithful use of tradition?

PRAYER

Commit what you have learned from God's Word in this lesson to prayer.

- Praise God for revealing His character and works to you through His written Word.
- Confess any ways in which you've neglected the Bible as a means of God's grace.
- Thank God for His promise to sanctify you as His Spirit works through His Word.
- Ask God to give you the same attitude toward His Word that Jesus had during His earthly life and ministry.

REVIEW QUIZ

Use these multiple-choice questions to measure what you learned from this lesson.

1. Dr. Ferguson observed that it is difficult for us to listen to the Word of God when we are filled with which of the following?
   a. Our career responsibilities
   b. Our personal opinions
   c. Our religious duties
   d. Our busy lives

2. Which of the following is the best definition of the word *correct* as it is used in the context of 2 Timothy 3:16?
   a. To note an error
   b. To tell someone his flaws
   c. To straighten what is malformed
   d. To point out a better way
3. Which of the following was *not* given as an example of how God's Word is profitable?
   a. It teaches what is true.
   b. It reproves what is false.
   c. It trains us in righteousness.
   d. It answers our dilemmas in detail.
4. In relation to how we should approach the Bible, which of the following did Dr. Ferguson say is a sign that one has truly become a Christian?
   a. He embraces God as Father.
   b. He yields to the Holy Spirit.
   c. He commits to serving Jesus Christ.
   d. He shuts his mouth before God.
5. When you study the Bible you should be asking God to reveal ways for you to improve yourself.
   a. True
   b. False
6. Which of the following was *not* given as a question to ask oneself when studying the Bible?
   a. What does the passage mean to me personally?
   b. How does my life fail to conform to this teaching?
   c. How can my character be corrected?
   d. What does the passage teach?

Answer Key—Means of Grace: God's Word

REFLECTION & DISCUSSION QUESTIONS

Before the Video

What Do You Think?

These are personal questions. The answers should be based on your own knowledge and experience.

Scripture Reading

- What is Scripture able to do? In what four ways is the Word of God profitable for believers?

  This passage states that Scripture is able to make one "wise for salvation through faith in Christ Jesus." Furthermore, God's Word is profitable for teaching, reproof, correction, and training in righteousness. Through His Word, God equips us for the good works for which we were created in Christ Jesus (Eph. 2:10).

During the Video

Powerful to Save

- What is the first reason why it is important to study Scripture and belong to a church where Scripture is faithfully expounded?

  The Bible is important because through it we are made wise for salvation through faith in Jesus Christ. Though the Bible itself does not save us, it is by means of the Bible that Christ the Savior is revealed to us through the Holy Spirit. If we do not look to the Jesus of the Bible, we are left with a Jesus of our own imaginations because our only access to who Jesus is in terms of His person and work is found in the pages of the Bible.

- How do people often discover the truth of Scripture?

  Most people discover the truth of Scripture through the people with whom God has surrounded them. There are cases where people are directly led to Scripture apart from others, but oftentimes, people are influenced by family members, friends, pastors, or others who point them to the Bible and the way of salvation in Jesus Christ.

- What is the second reason why studying Scripture is important for Christians?

  Scripture is vitally important because it speaks to us from the mouth of God. We are to think of the Bible as coming right from the heart of God to communicate His presence to us. When we read the Bible, we are hearing the voice of God.

Powerful to Sanctify

- What did George Whitefield do as an expression of the proper disposition of the Christian toward the Word of God?

  Whitefield read his Bible on his knees as an expression of submission to the Word of God. Just as when we kneel to pray, Whitefield's posture when reading the Word of God symbolizes the inward humility with which we are to approach the Word of God.

- What was called "the crying need in our generation"?

  Our generation needs to be humbled by the Word of God in order that it might produce godly character in us. Many polls show that the behavior of professing evangelical Christians does not differ much from the behavior of unbelievers. The Word of God should produce character in the Christian, just as a son has character produced in him as he listens to and watches his father.

- What is the third reason why Christians should study the Bible?

  The third reason why Christians should study the Bible is that it transforms the lives of the people of God. It's by having our minds renewed through the truth of Scripture that our emotions, affections, and lives are gloriously transformed. This is at the heart of what it is to serve the Lord because serving the Lord is fundamentally a matter of being a transformed individual.

After the Video

- What does it mean that the Bible is God-breathed?

  Second Timothy 3:16 is the only place in the New Testament where the Greek word that means "God-breathed" occurs. The Bible is God-breathed in the sense that when we read the Bible, we are actually listening to the voice of God Himself. We are to think of the Bible as coming right from the heart of God to communicate God's presence to us.

- How does the story of Jacob's wrestling with the angel of the Lord serve as a picture of the impact that the Scripture makes upon our lives?

  Genesis 32:22–32 narrates Jacob's encounter with God through a wrestling match with the angel of the Lord. Jacob refused to let go of the angel until the angel blessed him, and as a result of having met with God, Jacob walked away with a limp, humbled by his experience. Similarly, the Word of God should humble us and make us different as a result of our clinging to it.

- How would you respond to someone who says that we need traditions apart from the Bible to faithfully live the Christian life?

  Second Timothy 3:16–17 clearly states that God's Word contains all that we need to live the Christian life competently and to be equipped for every good work. Studying Scripture allows us to become familiar with the heartbeat of God, as He has revealed Himself in and through Scripture. Remembering 2 Timothy 3:16–17 may be very helpful when engaging a Roman Catholic who holds up tradition as on the same level as Scripture.

REVIEW QUIZ

Lesson 4

1. **B.**
There has been a shift over the years where people have become highly educated and have been encouraged to have personal opinions. This has resulted in a society that talks but hardly ever listens, both at the human level and in relation to God. Though other answer choices may be distractions, our own personal opinion was the option Dr. Ferguson noted.

2. **C.**
The Greek word for correct *was used outside of Scripture in a medical capacity. If someone had broken a bone, the physician would do what was necessary to enable its healing and to straighten it again. Likewise, as the Word is preached and as we absorb it, a transformation occurs in our souls to produce spiritual health.*

3. **D.**
God's Word teaches, reproves, corrects, and trains (2 Tim. 3:16). While it should provide principles to govern our personal decision-making, it does not provide detailed guidance for every situation—only the wisdom to think biblically about them.

4. **D.**
In this lesson, Roman 3:19 was referenced to introduce the idea that all those who realize their guilt before God shut their mouths. God's law reveals to us our failure to conform to it, and when the Holy Spirit enables us to realize this truth, we no longer seek to argue or defend ourselves before God or proclaim our own innocence or righteousness. That's why when we study the Bible, we should pray to God that we would listen to Him.

5. **B.**
The proper response to the Scripture is not to say, "Tell me what I have to do to improve," but, "Transform me." This is why Jesus prayed that the Father would sanctify us through His Word and not through what we do in and of ourselves.

6. **A.**
Because 2 Timothy 3:16 provides four purposes of the Bible as the inspired Word of God, we should ask the following questions when we study the Bible: What is the passage teaching? How is it reproving me? What needs to be corrected in my life? How can this train me in righteousness?

5

Means of Grace: Prayer

INTRODUCTION

Christians understand the tremendous privilege of being able to approach the Almighty God in prayer. Yet, too often this gift is taken for granted, misunderstood, or neglected. Knowing our human weaknesses and sinful tendencies, God has graciously provided us with guidance from His Word and assistance from His Spirit to help us pray rightly. In this lesson, Dr. Ferguson approaches the topic of prayer by looking at how Jesus taught His disciples to pray.

LEARNING GOALS

When you have finished this lesson, you should be able to:

- Identify the proper attitude in prayer and the proper approach to prayer
- Explain the meaning of each declaration and petition of the Lord's Prayer

KEY IDEAS

- Many Christians struggle in some degree in their prayer lives, but we should not be discouraged because the Holy Spirit will come to our help when we pray.
- Jesus provided His followers with a concrete model for prayer that gives us the proper attitude, approach, intimacy, and encouragement in our prayers to the Father.
- Effective prayer is inseparably linked to God's Word.

REFLECTION & DISCUSSION QUESTIONS

Before the Video

What Do You Think?

Take a moment to answer the following questions. They will prepare you for the lecture.

- How would you currently rate your prayer life on a scale of 1–10?

- What would you say is the greatest strength in your prayer life?

- If you could change one thing about your prayer life, what would it be and why?

Scripture Reading

Likewise the Spirit helps us in our weakness. For we do not know what to pray for as we ought, but the Spirit himself intercedes for us with groanings too deep for words. And he who searches hearts knows what is the mind of the Spirit, because the Spirit intercedes for the saints according to the will of God.

—Romans 8:26–27

- What comfort does this passage offer believers in the area of prayer?

During the Video

Answer the following questions while you watch the video. They will guide you through the lecture.

The Challenge of Prayer *0:00–8:27*

- What does the anecdote about the Christian publisher and the book on prayer indicate about most Christians' view of their prayer lives?

- What are some reasons that we should not be discouraged when it comes to prayer?

- The Lord's Prayer is more than a basic manual on prayer. What else is it a basic manual on?

The Model of Prayer *8:27–24:16*

- Where else in Scripture besides Luke 11 does the Lord's Prayer appear?

- In the Lord's Prayer, Jesus tells us to address God as our Father. When was the only time that Jesus did not refer to God as Father?

- What did the Reformers understand about prayer that is clearly communicated in the Lord's Prayer?

After the Video

Answer the following questions after you have finished the lecture. They will help you identify and summarize the major points.

- What two things begin to happen when someone knows God as his heavenly Father?

  If you are in a group, have the members discuss specific ways in which they have seen the truth of these two realities on display in their own lives. Is one of these more challenging to live out than the other, and if so, why?

- According to Dr. Ferguson, why do many people not pray for daily bread?

  If you are in a group, have the members discuss the following: What is the purpose for praying for daily bread? If someone were to struggle with praying this petition of the Lord's Prayer, how would you help them see other ways of thinking about it?

- What are we requesting, in essence, when we ask God to forgive us?

  If you are in a group, have the members discuss how understanding and remembering this truth should affect our attitude and approach when we ask God for forgiveness. In what ways is this truth sobering, and in what ways is it freeing?

PRAYER

Commit what you have learned from God's Word in this lesson to prayer.

- Praise God for His willingness to listen to your prayers as a Father.
- Confess the specific sins that hinder your prayer life, such as unbelief or pride.
- Thank God for the Holy Spirit's intercession for you in accord with God's will.
- Ask God to help you better use the model Jesus provided in the Lord's Prayer.

REVIEW QUIZ

Use these multiple-choice questions to measure what you learned from this lesson.

1. What is the context of the Lord's Prayer in the Sermon on the Mount?
   a. Knowing God as Creator
   b. Knowing God as Savior
   c. Knowing God as Ruler
   d. Knowing God as Father

2. When does God place Himself under obligation to answer our prayers?
   a. When we obey His Word
   b. When we pray for others
   c. When we appeal to His promises
   d. When we ask anything in Jesus' name

3. Asking God to give us our daily bread exemplifies a petition for which of the following?
   a. Power
   b. Protection
   c. Provision
   d. Purpose

4. Dr. Ferguson noted that we often don't pray because we don't realize which of the following about ourselves?
   a. We are busy.
   b. We are weak.
   c. We are worldly.
   d. We are distracted.

5. The Lord's Prayer is characterized by simple words and phrases.
   a. True
   b. False

6. What does the example of Elijah and his prayers teach us?
   a. It is critical for us to understand the love of God.
   b. It is critical for us to understand the power of God.
   c. It is critical for us to understand the promises of God.
   d. It is critical for us to understand the commands of God.

Answer Key—Means of Grace: Prayer

REFLECTION & DISCUSSION QUESTIONS

Before the Video

What Do You Think?

These are personal questions. The answers should be based on your own knowledge and experience.

Scripture Reading

- What comfort does this passage offer believers in the area of prayer?

  Sometimes, in our human weakness, we're not sure what to pray. In these situations, we are not left to ourselves. According to this passage, the Holy Spirit intercedes for us, and He always prays for us according to the will of God. It is a great comfort to believers to know that when we don't know what to pray, the Holy Spirit is praying on our behalf.

During the Video

The Challenge of Prayer

- What does the anecdote about the Christian publisher and the book on prayer indicate about most Christians' view of their prayer lives?

  The anecdote indicates that many Christians—including well-known pastors, leaders, and teachers—find prayer difficult and view their prayer lives as inadequate. As a result, not many would consider themselves experts in prayer or consider themselves models of faithful prayer.

- What are some reasons that we should not be discouraged when it comes to prayer?

  The knowledge that the Holy Spirit helps believers pray should serve as an encouragement to Christians. Another encouragement is the fact that Jesus' disciples—and even the Apostle Paul—found it difficult at times to know how to pray.

- The Lord's Prayer is more than a basic manual for prayer. What else is it a basic manual on?

  The Lord's Prayer also serves as basic manual on life and how to live for God's glory in order that we may learn what it means to pray. Prayer and life are not two separate entities—we live as we pray, and we pray as we live.

The Model of Prayer

- Where else in Scripture besides Luke 11 does the Lord's Prayer appear?

  The Lord's Prayer also appears in Matthew 6:9–13. In this context, the Lord's Prayer appears during Jesus' teaching in the Sermon on the Mount.

- In the Lord's Prayer, Jesus tells us to address God as our Father. When was the only time that Jesus did not refer to God as Father?

  The only time that Jesus did not refer to God as Father was in His prayer on the cross, when He cried out, "My God, my God, why have you forsaken me?" In that moment, He had no consciousness of His Father's love for Him, but only a consciousness of being forsaken in His humanity by His heavenly Father.

- What did the Reformers understand about prayer that is clearly communicated in the Lord's Prayer?

  In the Lord's Prayer, we are prompted to pray that God's will be done. In accordance with this, the Reformers understood that prayer must be directed by the Word of God. By knowing the Word of God, we can rightly pray according to God's will, which He is determined to accomplish, and according to God's promises, which He is committed to keep.

After the Video

- What two things begin to happen when someone knows God as his heavenly Father?

  When someone knows God as a heavenly Father, he begins to be delivered from hypocrisy. He does not have to pretend to be something that he is not because the Father already knows everything about him. Second, he begins to be delivered from anxiety. When someone knows God as his heavenly Father, he can be assured that God will take care of him as his Father.

- According to Dr. Ferguson, why do many people not pray for daily bread?

  Many people do not pray for daily bread because they consider themselves quite capable of providing it for themselves. They see little need to pray for daily bread when they have refrigerators and pantries filled with food.

- What are we requesting, in essence, when we ask God to forgive us?

  In this lesson, Dr. Ferguson enhanced our perspective on how to think about the petition of the Lord's Prayer, "Forgive us our sins" (Luke 11:4). When we ask God to forgive us, we are asking, in reality, that God would find someone else to pay our debt, that He would send His Son to die on the cross so that we will not have to die eternally in hell.

REVIEW QUIZ

Lesson 5

1. **D.**
The context of the Lord's Prayer in the Sermon on the Mount is knowing God as one's heavenly Father. When we truly embrace the truth that God is our Father, we are able to pray with the right attitude. Jesus' use of the phrase "Our Father" reveals that when we come to know Jesus Christ, His Father is our Father. Everything we see in Jesus' relationship with the Father is the relationship into which He invites us.

2. **C.**
The wonder of prayer is that the heavenly Father has placed Himself under obligation to fulfill the promises He has made in His Word. When we pray, we should come to God on the basis of His promises and ask that He would keep them. This is the prayer of faith referred to in the book of James (5:13–18).

3. **C.**
When we pray, "Give us this day our daily bread," we are confessing our need for daily provision and asking God to provide for us. This is a prayer for the blessing of God upon the necessities of our lives that will nourish us in such a way that we'll be able to live for His glory.

4. **B.**
Dr. Ferguson noted that this is the church's greatest problem in the West when it comes to prayer. We don't realize how weak we really are. We think that we can do everything ourselves, and that makes us prayerless. It is only when we realize how dependent on God we are that we learn to pray.

5. **A.**
The wording of the Lord's Prayer is not complex or difficult to understand. Jesus reduced the prayer to the absolute essentials, and it is accessible and understandable for all Christians. The Lord's Prayer shows us that God does not require us to use fancy or complicated language when we come to Him in prayer.

6. **C.**
Elijah's prayer that it would not rain in 1 Kings 17 was in accordance with God's promise that if His people rebelled, Israel would experience draught and famine in the land. For Israel's sake, Elijah prayed that God would be faithful to keep the promise He had made. Had Elijah not known the promises of God, he would have been unable to be the means through whom God fulfilled them.

6

Means of Grace: Baptism

INTRODUCTION

When Christians think about baptism, what often comes to mind is debate and controversy over how it should be administered and to whom it should be administered. But what is most important for us to understand is *why* God has given us the sign and seal of baptism. In this lecture, Dr. Ferguson explains the significance of the sacraments, provides a detailed look at the baptism of Jesus, and notes how Jesus' baptism sheds light on the meaning of our own baptism.

LEARNING GOALS

When you have finished this lesson, you should be able to:

- Understand why God has given signs and seals to His people
- Explain the significance of the sacrament of baptism

KEY IDEAS

- The sacraments of the New Testament serve as special signs and seals of the gospel.
- God's promises are accompanied by physical signs that testify to His promises, and as such, they are first and foremost not signs of our faith but signs of God's faithfulness.
- In baptism, we are identified and named as belonging to the family of God.

REFLECTION & DISCUSSION QUESTIONS

Before the Video

What Do You Think?

Take a moment to answer the following questions. They will prepare you for the lecture.

- When you were baptized, what did your baptism mean?

- How much have you thought about the significance of your baptism this week?

Scripture Reading

> *What shall we say then? Are we to continue in sin that grace may abound? By no means! How can we who died to sin still live in it? Do you not know that all of us who have been baptized into Christ Jesus were baptized into his death? We were buried therefore with him by baptism into death, in order that, just as Christ was raised from the dead by the glory of the Father, we too might walk in newness of life.*
>
> —Romans 6:1–4

- What should result in our lives when we are baptized into the death of Christ?

During the Video

Answer the following questions while you watch the video. They will guide you through the lecture.

The Significance of Signs *0:00–10:50*

- What are the two sacraments of the New Testament?

- In the Old Testament, what was the sign of promise to Noah? To Abraham?

The Significance of Baptism *10:50–23:31*

- When John baptized people in the Jordan, what did that baptism symbolize?

- Why did John not want to baptize Jesus?

- After quoting Matthew 28:18–20, how did Dr. Ferguson define baptism?

After the Video

Answer the following questions after you have finished the lecture. They will help you identify and summarize the major points.

- What are the sacraments first and foremost a sign of? What are they *not* primarily a sign of?

  If you are in a group, have the members discuss the significance of the distinction in the question above. What might be the result of confusing the two, and how could that negatively affect one's Christian life?

- How do people often give the wrong type of response to the question, "What did your baptism mean?"

  If you are in a group, have the members discuss their own responses to that same question in the "What Do You Think?" section. Do you tend to view your baptism simply in terms of something that you did in the past? In what ways did the teaching in this lecture help to change your perspective?

- As we seek to better understand the sacrament of baptism, why is it critical that we understand the meaning of Jesus' own baptism in the Jordan?

  If you are in a group, have members discuss the following statement from this lesson:

  > The River Jordan was full of the symbolism of the guilt of sinners. That's why Jesus said He needed to be baptized. Symbolically, Jesus is being baptized with waters of divine judgment. . . . He was really saying His baptism in the Jordan was a sign of His baptism for our sins on the cross of Calvary. That was the real baptism of which His baptism was a sign.

  Have you ever heard Jesus' baptism described in this way? How does this change your perspective about both Jesus' baptism and your own?

PRAYER

Commit what you have learned from God's Word in this lesson to prayer.

- Praise God for providing the means by which you can come into fellowship with Him and know Him.
- Confess any ways in which you have failed to grasp the significance of baptism in your daily Christian life.
- Thank God that Jesus was baptized in the name of sinners so that you could be baptized in the name of Jesus.

- Ask God to give you an increasing awareness of your new name and a new family through baptism.

REVIEW QUIZ

Use these multiple-choice questions to measure what you learned from this lesson.

1. Which of the following is true about God's signs?
   a. They prove God's existence.
   b. They are given because of our frailty.
   c. They make God's promise more trustworthy.
   d. They provide a means of salvation.
2. Circumcision was a sign of which of the following?
   a. Abraham's faith
   b. Abraham's obedience
   c. God's power in salvation
   d. God's gracious act of justification
3. Which of the following does baptism do?
   a. Transforms our hearts
   b. Forgives our sins
   c. Gives us a new name
   d. Grants us the Holy Spirit
4. When God gave Adam and Eve promises in the garden of Eden, what were the physical signs of those promises?
   a. Trees
   b. Animals
   c. Miracles
   d. Rainbows
5. When the first questions that people have about the sacraments are about fundamental issues, it's a sign that they've never really grasped the controversial issues.
   a. True
   b. False
6. Which of the following is true about baptism and the Lord's Supper?
   a. The water is mystically transformed.
   b. The signs point to a spiritual reality.
   c. The bread becomes the body of Christ.
   d. The wine becomes the blood of Christ.

Answer Key—Means of Grace: Baptism

REFLECTION & DISCUSSION QUESTIONS

Before the Video

What Do You Think?

These are personal questions. The answers should be based on your own knowledge and experience.

Scripture Reading

- What should result in our lives when we are baptized into the death of Christ?

  Our baptism into the death of Christ means that we have died to sin. Just as Christ was physically raised from the dead, believers are raised to live a new life—one that should result in the pursuit of holy and godly living in relation to both God and man.

During the Video

The Significance of Signs

- What are the two sacraments of the New Testament?

  The sacraments given by Christ for believers to observe are baptism and the Lord's Supper. These are not instruments that we use to obtain grace automatically; rather, they are instruments that God uses to bring us into fellowship with Himself. These sacraments serve as special signs and seals of the gospel.

- In the Old Testament, what was the sign of promise to Noah? To Abraham?

  God's promise to Noah that He would never again flood the earth was accompanied by the sign of a rainbow. Whenever Noah and his family saw a rainbow, it would serve as a reminder of this promise. When God made a covenant with Abraham, He gave to Abraham and his family the sign of circumcision. Circumcision was a sign of the righteousness that God gave to Abraham, which Abraham received through faith.

The Significance of Baptism

- When John baptized people in the Jordan, what did that baptism symbolize?

  John's baptism was a baptism of repentance for the forgiveness of sins (Mark 1:4; Luke 3:3). At its heart, it was a baptism for sinners to prepare them for the coming of the Lord. When people came to the Jordan to be baptized by John, the rite was symbolic of God's washing away their sin and guilt into the river. Dr. Ferguson said the symbolism was as such that it was almost as if the waters of the Jordan were full of the guilt of sinners.

- Why did John not want to baptize Jesus?

  As mentioned above, John's baptism was a baptism of repentance for the forgiveness of sins. Because Jesus was sinless, and therefore not in need of cleansing, John did not want to baptize Jesus. John did, however, obey Jesus' command to baptize Him, and Jesus' baptism was a sign of the work that He would do on the cross.

- After quoting Matthew 28:18–20, how did Dr. Ferguson define baptism?

  Dr. Ferguson defined baptism in the following way: "Baptism is a naming ceremony in which I, who have been reared in the family of Adam, am given the sign of the new family of Jesus Christ." The waters of baptism do nothing to transform our hearts, yet according to the teaching of the New Testament, being baptized means that a new family name is placed on us, and having that family name determines the whole course of our lives.

After the Video

- What are the sacraments first and foremost a sign of? What are they *not* primarily a sign of?

  The sacraments are first and foremost a sign of the gospel that draw from us the response of faith. They are not *primarily a sign of our response to God's Word or a sign of our faith. In other words, the sacraments are primarily about the work that God has done on our behalf, not about our own faith or what we do for Him.*

- How do people often give the wrong type of response to the question, "What did your baptism mean?"

  People often respond to this question by talking about themselves and what has happened in them. But according to the New Testament, baptism is not fundamentally about us, but rather, it's about what God has done for us in Christ. Baptism tells us who we are named after and belong to, and this has ethical implications, which is why Paul refers to baptism and its relationship to the Christian life in Romans 6.

- As we seek to better understand the sacrament of baptism, why is it critical that we understand the meaning of Jesus' own baptism in the Jordan?

  Jesus' baptism was symbolic of His taking on Himself the guilt of sinners, which He would do in reality in His true baptism on the cross when He died for our sins. That was His real baptism, of which His baptism in the Jordan was a sign. Understanding Jesus' baptism in this way helps us better understand Him as our substitute and what He did for us on the cross. Thus, it better helps us understand baptism as a sign of God's promise to us in Christ as opposed to a sign of our faith.

REVIEW QUIZ

Lesson 6

1. **B.**
   God understands our human frailty. He could have simply given us His Word alone, but He gave the signs to help us remember His promises. The sacraments do not make God's promises more trustworthy, because God's Word is trustworthy in and of itself. The sacraments also do not prove God's existence, and by participating in baptism or the Lord's Supper, we do not gain salvation. The instrument of our salvation is faith in the person and work of Christ alone.

2. **D.**
   Circumcision was a sign of God's gracious act of justification. It was not a sign of Abraham's faith but rather a sign of the righteousness that God gave to Abraham, which Abraham received through faith (see Rom. 4:11).

3. **C.**
   In baptism, we are identified as having a new name and belonging to a new family. Having that new name is a reminder of all that God has done for us in and through Jesus Christ and all that He is willing to do for us through the ministry of the Holy Spirit. The whole of the Christian life is to be lived in the context of this new name, and the whole of our Christian lives will also be determined by it.

4. **A.**
   God gave the Tree of Life and the Tree of Knowledge of Good and Evil to Adam and Eve as signs of His promises. The rainbow served as a sign of God's promise to Noah, and miracles served to show God's faithfulness to His Word at various stages in redemptive history.

5. **B.**
   The opposite is true: when people first want to discuss the controversial issues, it's a sign that they haven't grasped the fundamental issues concerning the sacraments. What is most important when it comes to the sacraments is that we understand why God has given us these physical realities and understand that God characteristically reveals Himself and His purposes by means of promises.

6. **B.**
   Baptism and the Lord's Supper are signs that point to a spiritual reality. The belief that the bread actually becomes the body of Christ and the wine actually becomes the blood of Christ in the Lord's Supper is the erroneous Roman Catholic belief known as transubstantiation. Further, there is nothing mystical about the water in which one is baptized.

7

Means of Grace: The Lord's Supper

INTRODUCTION

The Lord's Supper was instituted by Jesus before His death and subsequent resurrection. Though Christians are familiar with this practice and have likely taken the Lord's Supper many times, how deeply is the meaning of this sacrament truly understood? In this lecture, Dr. Ferguson discusses seven aspects of the Lord's Supper to help believers gain a deeper biblical understanding and insight into the supper's true meaning and significance.

LEARNING GOALS

When you have finished this lesson, you should be able to:

- Understand the meaning and significance of the Lord's Supper
- List and explain the seven aspects of the Lord's Supper

KEY IDEAS

- The Lord's Supper is one of the two sacraments instituted in the New Testament.
- The Lord's Supper, as a sacrament, points us to Jesus Christ, what He has done for us, and what it means to have fellowship with Him.
- There are seven words that can be used to summarize the Lord's Supper according to Paul's teaching in 1 Corinthians 11: commemoration, proclamation, benediction, communion, consecration, repetition, and anticipation.
- Properly understanding the Lord's Supper will naturally lead us to examine ourselves.

REFLECTION & DISCUSSION QUESTIONS

Before the Video

What Do You Think?

Take a moment to answer the following questions. They will prepare you for the lecture.

- Do you remember when you first began taking the Lord's Supper, and if so, does anything stand out in your mind about that experience?

- Is it biblically permissible to use elements other than bread and wine in the Lord's Supper? Why or why not, and where does one draw the line?

Scripture Reading

When you come together, it is not the Lord's supper that you eat. For in eating, each one goes ahead with his own meal. One goes hungry, another gets drunk. What! Do you not have houses to eat and drink in? Or do you despise the church of God and humiliate those who have nothing? What shall I say to you? Shall I commend you in this? No, I will not.

—1 Corinthians 11:20–22

- In what ways was the Corinthian church not properly celebrating the Lord's Supper?

During the Video

Answer the following questions while you watch the video. They will guide you through the lecture.

Introduction to the Lord's Supper *0:00–6:37*

- Where in the New Testament do we find the most condensed teaching on the Lord's Supper?

- Both baptism and the Lord's Supper are weighted with what kind of significance?

Characteristics of the Lord's Supper *6:37–23:04*

- What Old Testament example does Dr. Ferguson give that clarifies the proper attitude to have when taking the Lord's Supper?

- Seven words are used to characterize different aspects of the Lord's Supper. What is the significance of each one of these characteristics?

Commemoration:

Proclamation:

Benediction:

Communion:

Consecration:

Repetition:

Anticipation:

After the Video

Answer the following questions after you have finished the lecture. They will help you identify and summarize the major points.

- What is wrong with approaching the Lord's Supper as if one has to work up pious feelings about Jesus?

If you are in a group, have the members discuss whether they have come to the Lord's Supper in the belief that they needed to contribute or produce something. Why do you think that people might have a tendency to do this?

- Should the Lord's Supper be an individualistic experience? Why or why not?

If you are in a group, have the members discuss whether they've primarily viewed the Lord's Supper more individually or corporately. Does Paul address the Corinthian church in 1 Corinthians 11:23–32 in more individual or corporate terms? How so?

- In what ways is the Lord's Supper an anticipation?

If you are in a group, have the members discuss the following questions: On a daily basis, how deeply do you yearn for the return of Christ and the new heavens and new earth? What are some ways that you might cultivate a love for the life to come over this present life? Do you find that you yearn for the eternal state more when things are going badly for you, and not as much when things are good? Why might this be the case?

PRAYER

Commit what you have learned from God's Word in this lesson to prayer.

- Praise God for providing the sacraments as a means of grace.
- Confess times when you have taken lightly the privilege of the Lord's Supper.
- Thank God for the full meal that you will someday enjoy in Christ's presence that is anticipated in the Lord's Supper.
- Ask God to cultivate a deeper love and appreciation for the Lord's Supper through His Spirit that it might naturally lead to godly self-examination.

REVIEW QUIZ

Use these multiple-choice questions to measure what you learned from this lesson.

1. When Jesus says, "Do this in remembrance of me," which aspect of the Lord's Supper is being noted?
    a. Proclamation
    b. Commemoration
    c. Consecration
    d. Benediction

2. Who is the host of the Lord's Supper?
    a. Elders
    b. Deacons
    c. Jesus Christ
    d. Congregations

3. Why did the Corinthian church need to be taught that the Lord's Supper involves consecration?
    a. The church was neglecting to take the Lord's Supper.
    b. The church was using elements other than bread and wine.
    c. The church was allowing unbelievers to take the Lord's Supper.
    d. The church was also participating in pagan feasts involving idolatry.

4. How frequently should a church take the Lord's Supper?
    a. Often
    b. Weekly
    c. Quarterly
    d. Infrequently

5. In Roman Catholic theology, the bread and wine of the Lord's Supper transform into the body and blood of Jesus.
   a. True
   b. False
6. A proper understanding of the Lord's Supper will naturally lead to which of the following?
   a. Self-esteem
   b. Self-deprecation
   c. Self-examination
   d. Self-actualization

Answer Key—
Means of Grace: The Lord's Supper

REFLECTION & DISCUSSION QUESTIONS

Before the Video

What Do You Think?

These are personal questions. The answers should be based on your own knowledge and experience.

Scripture Reading

- In what ways was the Corinthian church not properly celebrating the Lord's Supper?

  People in the church would take the Lord's Supper on their own and not wait for others. Some would drink to excess and become drunk. Others who lacked financial means would go hungry and not be able to take the supper at all. All of this evidenced that the church had a lack of care and concern for fellow members of the body, and that there was disunity among them.

During the Video

Introduction to the Lord's Supper

- Where in the New Testament do we find the most condensed teaching on the Lord's Supper?

  First Corinthians 10–11 contains the most condensed teaching on the Lord's Supper. The Corinthian church needed much correction from the Apostle Paul in many areas of the Christian life, including how they celebrated the Lord's Supper, so Paul addressed their issues in 1 Corinthians 10:14–22; 11:23–32 about what it really means to come to the Lord's Table to partake of Christ.

- Both baptism and the Lord's Supper are weighted with what kind of significance?

  Both baptism and the Lord's Supper are weighted with theological and Christological significance. They point to Jesus Christ, what He has done for us, and what it means to enjoy fellowship with Him. This is particularly evident in Paul's teaching on the Lord's Supper in 1 Corinthians 10–11.

Characteristics of the Lord's Supper

- What Old Testament example does Dr. Ferguson give that clarifies the proper attitude to have when taking the Lord's Supper?

Dr. Ferguson referenced the event in Numbers 21:4–9 when Moses, as God had commanded, made a bronze serpent so that the Israelites in the wilderness might be saved from the snake bites that they received on account of their sin. As the Israelites looked to the bronze serpent in order to be saved, so believers today look to Christ and the salvation that He alone provides to us. This makes Christ the primary focus of the Lord's Supper as a commemoration, and not ourselves.

- Seven words are used to characterize different aspects of the Lord's Supper. What is the significance of each one of these characteristics?

  Commemoration: *The Lord's Supper focuses on the work Christ has accomplished.*

  Proclamation: *The Lord's Supper visibly preaches the gospel of Jesus Christ.*

  Benediction: *The Lord's Supper is God's word of blessing to us in Christ.*

  Communion: *The Lord's Supper is a participation in the body and blood of Christ, who as a host has invited us to His table to partake of the gift of His person.*

  Consecration: *The Lord's Supper reconsecrates us in devotion to the Lord Jesus Christ.*

  Repetition: *The Lord's Supper is to be celebrated often because we need the fellowship with Christ.*

  Anticipation: *The Lord's Supper fills us with a sense of anticipation for the return of our Lord and Savior Jesus Christ and our presence with Him eternally.*

After the Video

- What is wrong with approaching the Lord's Supper as if one has to work up pious feelings about Jesus?

  This reveals a mind-set that is more focused on what a person does for God rather than what God has done for the person through Jesus Christ. Celebrating the Lord's Supper should remind us that all the resources of our salvation are not to be found in ourselves, or even in our own faith, but in Jesus Christ.

- Should the Lord's Supper be an individualistic experience? Why or why not?

  While each person is called to examine himself when taking the Lord's Supper, it is meant to be a corporate celebration. Dr. Ferguson notes that the Lord's Supper is meant to be the congregation's preaching of the gospel to one another without the use of words. This reality is intimately tied to our understanding of the sacraments as signs of God's promise to us in Christ, symbolic of the gospel.

- In what ways is the Lord's Supper an anticipation?

  The bread and wine of the Lord's Supper anticipate the full meal that believers will enjoy one day in the eternal kingdom. Dr. Ferguson notes that in a sense, the small morsels of bread and tastes of wine in the Lord's Supper are designed by God to show us that this is not the full meal—the full meal is coming in the future when we will enjoy it in the presence of God with all His saints.

REVIEW QUIZ

Lesson 7

1. **B.**
The commemorative aspect of the Lord's Supper means that we take the Lord's Supper in order to remember Christ and what He has accomplished on our behalf. The fact that the Lord's Supper is a commemoration underlines for us that all of the resources of our salvation are not to be found in ourselves or our faith, but only in Jesus Christ.

2. **C.**
Jesus is the host of the Lord's Supper. When we come to the Lord's Table, the emphasis should not so much be on what we are doing as it is on the person we are enjoying. He is the host, and He has invited us to His table to enjoy the gift of His presence.

3. **D.**
Paul deals with issues surrounding the Lord's Supper in two places in 1 Corinthians. In the first instance (10:14–22), Paul is dealing with the Corinthian practice of attending pagan feasts. For this reason, Paul underscores how the Lord's Supper requires consecration, such that believers must turn away from paganism and idolatry.

4. **A.**
The Bible does not explicitly mandate how often the sacrament of the Lord's Supper should be observed. However, Jesus anticipated that the church would observe it often in remembrance of Him (1 Cor. 11:23–25). Dr. Ferguson did not make an argument for a specific frequency but only for the regularity of the Lord's Supper. This is because we, as Christians, need this time of fellowship with our Savior.

5. **A.**
The Roman Catholic Church believes and teaches that the elements of bread and wine transform into the body and blood of Christ, a belief known as transubstantiation. The Reformed view maintains that the bread and wine remain truly bread and wine, and Christ is really, but spiritually, present and received by faith.

6. **C.**
When we properly understand the Lord's Supper, we will naturally be led to self-examination. Dr. Ferguson reflected that such an understanding will lead us to say, "Lord, there is nothing in me that makes me worthy of communion with You, but there is everything in Your grace that calls me to have communion with You, to know Your presence, to enjoy Your grace, and to trust You now until eternity."

8

Facing the Enemy

INTRODUCTION

Becoming a Christian means being transferred from the kingdom of darkness to the kingdom of light. When this happens, Christians also gain a new enemy and adversary: Satan. It's easy for Christians to err in one of two ways when it comes to the devil. On the one hand, we can focus on him too much, and on the other, we can fail to recognize the power of his influence. In this lecture, Dr. Ferguson describes the nature of our enemy, as well as the resources at our disposal to fight against him.

LEARNING GOALS

When you have finished this lesson, you should be able to:

- Understand the nature of the battle that Christians face
- Identify and describe the characteristics of our adversary the devil
- List the resources available for Christians to engage in spiritual warfare

KEY IDEAS

- Though Christ has won the decisive battle against the devil, Christians will still experience spiritual warfare until the enemy's final defeat.
- As Christians, we have to know the nature of the battle against evil and the characteristics of the devil if we are to remain standing against his schemes.
- Believers can take confidence in the resources provided in Christ for victory in the battle against the devil, assured that the battle has already been won.

REFLECTION & DISCUSSION QUESTIONS

Before the Video

What Do You Think?

Take a moment to answer the following questions. They will prepare you for the lecture.

- Has your life been easier or more difficult since you became a Christian? Explain.

- What are Satan's strategies? List as many as you can.

Scripture Reading

Finally, be strong in the Lord and in the strength of his might. Put on the whole armor of God, that you may be able to stand against the schemes of the devil. For we do not wrestle against flesh and blood, but against the rulers, against the authorities, against the cosmic powers over this present darkness, against the spiritual forces of evil in the heavenly places. Therefore take up the whole armor of God, that you may be able to withstand in the evil day, and having done all, to stand firm.

—Ephesians 6:10–13

- According to this passage, how serious is spiritual warfare, and what words and phrases in the passage support your answer?

During the Video

Answer the following questions while you watch the video. They will guide you through the lecture.

The Nature of the Battle *0:00–9:57*

- Where is the Christian's battle against the spiritual forces of evil being fought?

- How does Dr. Ferguson understand the phrase "the evil day"?

The Character of the Enemy *9:57–17:23*

- What is the first thing Paul reveals about the character of our enemy?

- How does Dr. Ferguson describe the disposition of the devil? What title does Paul give him that brings our attention to his disposition?

The Resources for Victory *17:23–23:53*

- When Paul uses the analogy of battle gear, what does he have in mind?

- What does the breastplate of righteousness guard against?

After the Video

Answer the following questions after you have finished the lecture. They will help you identify and summarize the major points.

- In Ephesians, what topic immediately precedes the section on spiritual warfare, and what is the connection between the two?

  If you are in a group, have the members discuss the following: Do you tend to think of relational struggles as spiritual battles and as something that Satan may be influencing? How might arming yourself with this way of thinking better help you when you experience conflict?

- What characteristic of Satan was apparent in his interaction with Eve in the garden of Eden?

  If you are in a group, have the members list as many examples as they can think of regarding how Satan deceives us. What are some practical strategies for recognizing Satan's lies?

- In Ephesians 6:11, 13, and 14, what word does Paul repeatedly use to describe the Christian's goal in spiritual battle?

  If you are in a group, have the members discuss the following: Does this command from Paul strike you as something easy to accomplish or difficult? Why? What do you think is required to be able to stand?

PRAYER

Commit what you have learned from God's Word in this lesson to prayer.

- Praise God that Jesus triumphed over the devil in the cross.
- Confess any arrogant pride that leaves you susceptible to deception.
- Thank God that you have been delivered from the kingdom of darkness.
- Ask God to arm you with the spiritual weapons to fight against the Evil One.

REVIEW QUIZ

Use these multiple-choice questions to measure what you learned from this lesson.

1. Which of the following is true after becoming a Christian?
   a. Life gets easier.
   b. Life stays the same.
   c. Life becomes more difficult.
   d. Life becomes perfect.
2. When Paul says that our battle is "not against flesh and blood," this refers to which characteristic of Satan?
   a. He is evil.
   b. He is fallen.
   c. He is eternal.
   d. He is supernatural.
3. The fact that there are rulers, authorities, and cosmic powers refers to which of the following truths about the character of our enemy?
   a. He will be cast into the lake of fire.
   b. He rebelled against God.
   c. He tempts mankind.
   d. He is well organized in strategy.
4. Which piece of spiritual armor is "the readiness given by the gospel of peace"?
   a. Breastplate
   b. Helmet
   c. Shoes
   d. Sword
5. There is no spiritual profit in thinking about Satan or his demons.
   a. True
   b. False
6. In order to wear the belt of truth, what is involved in addition to knowing the truth of the gospel?
   a. Teaching the truth to others
   b. Exposing false teachers and churches
   c. Receiving the truth of the gospel in our hearts
   d. Acting in accordance with the truth

Answer Key—Facing the Enemy

REFLECTION & DISCUSSION QUESTIONS

Before the Video

What Do You Think?

These are personal questions. The answers should be based on your own knowledge and experience.

Scripture Reading

- According to this passage, how serious is spiritual warfare, and what words and phrases in the passage support your answer?

  This passage makes it clear that spiritual warfare is a serious issue in the believer's life. It is so serious that it requires "the strength of his might" and not our own strength, for we wrestle against "the spiritual forces of evil," face "the evil day," and require "the whole armor of God" to "stand against the schemes of the devil."

During the Video

The Nature of the Battle

- Where is the Christian's battle against the spiritual forces of evil being fought?

  The Christian's battle against the spiritual forces of evil is being fought "in the heavenly places." This phrase also appears in Ephesians 1, which says that we are blessed in Christ with every spiritual blessing "in the heavenly places." Paul uses this same expression at the beginning and end of Ephesians to show that Christians are brought into a new realm, "the heavenly places," but that is also the very realm in which we engage in conflict.

- How does Dr. Ferguson understand the phrase "the evil day"?

  Dr. Ferguson presented "the evil day" as a time when we are both spiritually weak and have sinful desires. That combination of weakness and sinful desire is when we are most liable to fall prey to Satan's temptations.

The Character of the Enemy

- What is the first thing Paul reveals about the character of our enemy?

  The first thing Paul reveals about the character of our enemy is that he is spiritual in nature. Because the devil is spiritual and supernatural in power, he needs to be dealt with using spiritual weapons, which is why prayer is a vitally important weapon in spiritual warfare with him.

- How does Dr. Ferguson describe the disposition of the devil? What title does Paul give him that brings our attention to this disposition?

  Dr. Ferguson described the disposition of the devil as evil. This is one of the devil's characteristics that Christians may have the hardest time grasping. Paul gives the devil the title "the evil one" (Eph. 6:16), suggesting that the devil is so evil that he is to be equated with evil itself.

The Resources for Victory

- When Paul uses the analogy of battle gear, what does he have in mind?

  When we read the passage about the Christian's spiritual weapons, it is important to remember that Roman soldiers did not guard a prisoner like Paul in full battle dress, so Paul is using the picture of the Roman soldier to remind us of another soldier in Scripture. Paul has in mind a prophecy of Isaiah, where Isaiah speaks about the Lord Himself wearing armor in the battle against Satan (Isa. 59:17).

- What does the breastplate of righteousness guard against?

  We need the breastplate of righteousness because Satan characteristically seeks to make us despair of our salvation by reminding us of our guilt and sin. He tempts us to think that, given the sin in our lives, we can't possibly be saved. But the truth is that Christians are righteous in Jesus Christ, and we must learn to wear the breastplate of His righteousness.

After the Video

- In Ephesians, what topic immediately precedes the section on spiritual warfare, and what is the connection between the two?

  The section on spiritual warfare is preceded by Paul's teaching on daily life about the relationships within the family between husbands and wives and parents and children. He also discusses broader societal relationships between masters and servants. These are connected in that these ordinary spheres of life are where we most often face spiritual battles. It is within the context of our ordinary lives that Satan seeks to defeat us, because it is within the context of our ordinary lives that God wants to use us to manifest His glory.

- What characteristic of Satan was apparent in his interaction with Eve in the garden of Eden?

  Satan's interactions with Eve in the garden reveal that he is a deceiver. As a result, the New Testament repeatedly tells us that we need to understand the truth of the gospel so that we are not deceived as Eve was. Many people's lives are in spiritual ruin because they have failed to understand that one of Satan's strategies is deception.

- In Ephesians 6:11, 13, and 14, what word does Paul repeatedly use to describe the Christian's goal in spiritual battle?

Paul repeatedly instructs his listeners to stand. *This may seem to be a simple command, and one might expect that Scripture would call us to something that sounds more significant. However, when we fully understand the weakness of our own flesh and the relentless assaults of the world and the devil, we realize that it is only by the grace of God that we have the ability to stand in the evil day.*

REVIEW QUIZ

Lesson 8

1. **C.**
   Life becomes more difficult after becoming a Christian because we gain a new enemy—one who is entirely evil and bent on our destruction. When we were unbelievers and enemies of God, we were "following the prince of the power of the air" and "by nature children of wrath" (Eph. 2:2–3). Satan had no reason to war against us when we were unbelievers. It is only when we become children of God that we become Satan's enemy.

2. **D.**
   The fact that our battle is not against flesh and blood tells us that Satan is supernatural in his power. When things go awry in the Christian life or in the church, we must always have at least one eye open to the presence and power of the enemy. This is why prayer is so important: spiritual enemies must be dealt with using spiritual weapons.

3. **D.**
   These differing levels and designations point out the fact that Satan is well organized in his strategy. It is not necessarily profitable to try to parse out the difference between "rulers," "authorities," and "cosmic powers." The main point of Scripture in using these terms is to indicate that a structure exists in the kingdom of darkness.

4. **C.**
   Paul encourages us to put on as shoes for our feet "the readiness given by the gospel of peace." Roman roads were narrow and dangerous, and walking on that kind of terrain required stable and strong shoes. This analogy of shoes as the readiness given by gospel of peace would have been especially significant to Paul's original audience. They would have understood that Paul was saying that the gospel provides believers with the peace of stability.

5. **B.**
   Christians must be aware of their enemy, Satan, and also be aware of his strategies, in order to thrive spiritually. To disregard him altogether is to put oneself in a dangerous position. Christians can err by making too much of Satan and his demons—even to the point that they do not take responsibility for their own sin. However, the proper reaction is not to disregard Satan altogether but to be mindful of who he is and how he seeks to deceive us.

6. **C.**
   The truth of the gospel in and of itself will not be profitable unless it is received in our hearts and embraced through faith. Through this, we are enabled to wage spiritual warfare, for Scripture will become so much a part of our lives that it holds everything around us together.

9

Discovering God's Will

INTRODUCTION

"What is God's will for my life?" Most Christians have asked this question at some point. In a world filled with a seemingly endless array of options, opportunities, and personal crossroads, how can Christians choose a path that is pleasing to the Lord? In this lesson, Dr. Ferguson demystifies the confusion surrounding the will of God and provides practical assistance to those who desire to walk according to it.

LEARNING GOALS

When you have finished this lesson, you should be able to:

- Understand the three ways in which God gives us guidance in Scripture
- Consider seven questions when seeking to make God-honoring decisions

KEY IDEAS

- Our task as Christians is to discover what the revealed will of God is and not what the secret will of God is.
- Our ability to discern the will of God is related to our understanding of Scripture, and our application of Scripture is related to our growth in Christian maturity.
- There are seven questions we can ask to help us make decisions when we are unclear as to what to do: (1) Is it lawful? (2) Is this action beneficial to me and to others? (3) Will it be enslaving? (4) Is this absolutely consistent with Christ's lordship? (5) Will this be helpful to others? (6) Is this course of action going to be consistent with biblical example? (7) Is this going to be consistent with the promotion of the glory of God?

REFLECTION & DISCUSSION QUESTIONS

Before the Video

What Do You Think?

Take a moment to answer the following questions. They will prepare you for the lecture.

- What is one of the most difficult decisions you've ever had to make? What resources did you use to help you go about making that decision?

- What counsel would you give to someone who asked you about how to know God's will regarding where they should attend college, whom they should marry, or what career they should pursue?

Scripture Reading

And so, from the day we heard, we have not ceased to pray for you, asking that you may be filled with the knowledge of his will in all spiritual wisdom and understanding, so as to walk in a manner worthy of the Lord, fully pleasing to him, bearing fruit in every good work and increasing in the knowledge of God.

—Colossians 1:9–10

- According to this passage, what should occur as a result of knowing the will of God?

During the Video

Answer the following questions while you watch the video. They will guide you through the lecture.

God's Will in Principle *0:00–10:05*

- Who is Epaphras? What did he pray for the church at Colossae?

- According to this lesson and Deuteronomy 29:29, what must Christians avoid?

God's Will in Practice *10:05–23:08*

- What do Hebrews 8 and 10 tell us about one of the roles of the Holy Spirit? Why is this significant?

- What does Dr. Ferguson suggest is the real problem faced by those who are concerned with finding out the secret will of God?

After the Video

Answer the following questions after you have finished the lecture. They will help you identify and summarize the major points.

- Why do many Christians tend to want to know the secret will of God? What would be the result of knowing God's secret will?

  If you are in a group, have the members discuss the following: Would life be better and easier if God told us exactly what to do (i.e., where to live, whether and whom to marry, what career to pursue, etc.)? Why or why not?

- Why were Christian books on the subject of discovering the will of God not prevalent before the eighteenth century?

  If you are in a group, have the members discuss the following: Is there value in reading books on the will of God? Why or why not? Would it be better to simply spend time reading God's Word directly? Why or why not?

- Of the seven questions a person should ask when seeking to make a God-honoring decision, which were most outstanding, personally applicable, or thought-provoking?

  If you are in a group, have the members discuss their answers to the above question. Which questions do you consistently consider when decision-making? Which ones do you often neglect to consider?

PRAYER

Commit what you have learned from God's Word in this lesson to prayer.

- Praise God that He has revealed His law in His Word and has written it on your heart by the Holy Spirit.
- Confess any major decisions you have made apart from considering the revealed will of God in Scripture.
- Thank God that even your missteps and mistakes are under His sovereign hand.
- Ask God to grant you, as Epaphras prayed for the church at Colossae, maturity and full assurance in all the will of God.

REVIEW QUIZ

Use these multiple-choice questions to measure what you learned from this lesson.

1. What book of the Bible is a book of precepts?
   a. Exodus
   b. Deuteronomy
   c. Psalms
   d. Proverbs

2. What would happen if God directly told believers all decisions they should make?
   a. We would always obey Him.
   b. We would not grow to maturity.
   c. We would be more pleasing to Him.
   d. We would experience greater spiritual growth.

3. According to the lesson, which characteristic of God particularly should ease our anxiety when seeking to make good decisions?
   a. He is our Judge.
   b. He is our Creator.
   c. He is our Redeemer.
   d. He is our Shepherd.

4. Why were catechisms helpful in teaching people how to discern the will of God?
   a. They required people to use their memory.
   b. They were in question-and-answer format.
   c. They expounded on the Ten Commandments.
   d. They outlined how to discover God's secret will.

5. "How can I discern the will of God?" The answer to this question is definite in the sense we can discover the revealed will of God for our lives in Scripture.
   a. True
   b. False

6. Which of the following is *not* one of the seven questions to ask when making decisions?
   a. Will this be helpful to others?
   b. Is it lawful?
   c. Is it enjoyable?
   d. Will it be enslaving?

Answer Key—Discovering God's Will

REFLECTION & DISCUSSION QUESTIONS

Before the Video

What Do You Think?

These are personal questions. The answers should be based on your own knowledge and experience.

Scripture Reading

- According to this passage, what should occur as a result of knowing the will of God?

  The purpose of knowing God's will is that we might walk before Him in a worthy manner, be fully pleasing to Him, bear fruit as we do good works, and increase in our knowledge of Him.

During the Video

God's Will in Principle

- Who is Epaphras? What did he pray for the church at Colossae?

  Epaphras may have been the man who brought the gospel to Colossae, and he may have been one of the pastors of the church. He and Paul had spent time praying together for the church at Colossae. In Colossians 4:12, we read from Paul, "Epaphras, who is one of you, a servant of Christ Jesus, greets you, always struggling on your behalf in his prayers, that you may stand mature and fully assured in all the will of God."

- According to this lesson and Deuteronomy 29:29, what must Christians avoid?

  Christians must avoid seeking to know the secret things of God. Instead, we must focus on what He has chosen to reveal to us in His Word, that we might be diligent to obey Him. It can be tempting as Christians to want to know the reasons for the circumstances of our lives. We must trust that God has good reasons that He has chosen not to reveal to us, and instead we must focus on His character and what He has already revealed to us in Scripture.

God's Will in Practice

- What do Hebrews 8 and 10 tell us about one of the roles of the Holy Spirit? Why is this significant?

  Hebrews 8 and 10 both quote from the prophecy of the new covenant found in Jeremiah 31, in which it is promised that the Holy Spirit will write God's law on our hearts. This is a wonderful principle for Christians to remember: God has already given directives that govern most of our Christian lives, and we should appreciate the directives that God has given to us and seek wisdom to apply them.

- What does Dr. Ferguson suggest is the real problem faced by those who are concerned with finding out the secret will of God?

  Many of those concerned with finding out the secret will of God in order to know what to do in various situations have a real problem rooted in ignorance of the Bible and the precepts that God has given to us with clarity in it. One of the best things we can do for ourselves in order to know the will of God in our circumstances is to know our Bibles.

After the Video

- Why do many Christians tend to want to know the secret will of God? What would be the result of knowing God's secret will?

  It was observed that many Christians tend to want to know the secret will of God because they assume that it would make their lives much easier. We would not have responsibility or any difficult decisions to make. However, if this were the case, we would never mature as believers because we would not need to make decisions that are pleasing to God. This is why we need, as Christians, to resist the urge to seek after knowledge of the secret will of God.

- Why were Christian books on the subject of discovering the will of God not prevalent before the eighteenth century?

  Previous to the eighteenth century, the church was primarily focused on teaching through various catechisms. Between 30 and 40 percent of these catechisms are comprised of questions about the Ten Commandments. Because people were being taught God's revealed will so completely and developing a biblical lens for viewing life, there was little need to have specific resources about everyday decision-making.

- Of the seven questions a person should ask when seeking to make a God-honoring decision, which were most outstanding, personally applicable, or thought provoking?

  The answer to this question will vary based on which questions discussed in this lecture stood out to you the most. The seven questions were: (1) Is it lawful? (2) Is this action beneficial to me and to others? (3) Will it be enslaving? (4) Is this absolutely consistent with Christ's lordship? (5) Will this be helpful to others? (6) Is this course of action going to be consistent with biblical example? (7) Is this going to be consistent with the promotion of the glory of God?

REVIEW QUIZ

Lesson 9

1. **D.**
The book of Proverbs is filled with precepts. In Proverbs, the great principles of knowing God's will are expounded. Many of the proverbs teach us what to do in certain situations and are the wise application of the law of God. In this lesson, Dr. Ferguson used the term directives *to refer to the law as the revelation of God's will, which is found in the books of Exodus and Deuteronomy.*

2. **B.**
While the idea of God's directly telling us what choices to make might sound appealing, this would not allow us to experience growth and maturity, which is His desire for us. Instead, we would be like a teenager who has never had any responsibility or decisions to make and, as a result, becomes dysfunctional and immature as an adult. God desires our spiritual maturity, and part of reaching that maturity involves seeking to make biblical and godly decisions.

3. **D.**
Because the Lord is our Shepherd, we need not fear when we have decisions to make. He has promised to lead and guide us, and He will always watch over and take care of His sheep. Christians can have every confidence that, although the Lord wants us to grow to maturity and exercise discernment in our decisions, He has promised that He will be with us and guide us through them.

4. **C.**
God has revealed His will to us through His Word in the Bible. Creeds, confessions, and catechisms seek to be accurate summaries of what has been revealed in Scripture. For this reason, many catechisms expound on the Ten Commandments, which could occupy between 30 and 40 percent of a catechism's teaching.

5. **A.**
"How can I discern the will of God?" The answer to this question is both definite and indefinite. It is definite in the sense that Scripture tells us God's revealed will, but it is indefinite in the sense that Scripture—apart from giving us directives, precepts, and principles for making every decision—does not tell us precisely what we should do in every unique circumstance.

6. **C.**
The seven questions were: (1) Is it lawful? (2) Is this action beneficial to me and to others? (3) Will it be enslaving? (4) Is this absolutely consistent with Christ's lordship? (5) Will this be helpful to others? (6) Is this course of action going to be consistent with biblical example? (7) Is this going to be consistent with the promotion of the glory of God? There is nothing inherently wrong with wanting to make decisions that will lead to enjoyment. However, one should ensure that all of these seven questions have the right answer first.

10

Enduring Hardships

INTRODUCTION

Christians are not exempt from the hardships and difficulties of this life. In fact, they often experience more suffering than those who do not profess Christ. When Christians fail to understand this reality, they can be easily deceived by those who falsely teach that all God wants for them is health, wealth, and happiness. In this lecture, Dr. Ferguson presents the true biblical view of suffering by examining the book of Hebrews.

LEARNING GOALS

When you have finished this lesson, you should be able to:

- Understand the true biblical perspective on suffering
- List and explain three important concepts about suffering from the book of Hebrews

KEY IDEAS

- It is important to realize a general principle at the beginning of the Christian life: the Christian life involves hardships.
- Jesus Christ endured hardships, so suffering is a means by which God conforms us to the image of Christ.
- Through our endurance and God's discipline, we develop character and are made to share in His holiness.

REFLECTION & DISCUSSION QUESTIONS

Before the Video

What Do You Think?

Take a moment to answer the following questions. They will prepare you for the lecture.

- Does God want all Christians to be healthy and wealthy? Why or why not?

- Is suffering good or bad? Explain your answer.

Scripture Reading

Therefore, since we are surrounded by so great a cloud of witnesses, let us also lay aside every weight, and sin which clings so closely, and let us run with endurance the race that is set before us, looking to Jesus, the founder and perfecter of our faith, who for the joy that was set before him endured the cross, despising the shame, and is seated at the right hand of God.

—Hebrews 12:1–2

- What should Christians do to be able to run their race with endurance? What hope does this passage set forth regarding the end result of such endurance?

During the Video

Answer the following questions while you watch the video. They will guide you through the lecture.

Perspectives on Suffering *0:00–12:01*

- What is the non-Christian view of suffering?

- What is the meaning of the word *endurance*?

Purposes of Suffering *12:01–23:12*

- According to Dr. Ferguson, what is one of the tragedies of our modern society?

- What Old Testament book does the author of Hebrews quote from when discussing the topic of discipline in Hebrews 12?

After the Video

Answer the following questions after you have finished the lecture. They will help you identify and summarize the major points.

- What were some of the difficulties that the recipients of the letter to the Hebrews were facing?

  If you are in a group, compare and contrast the sufferings of the original audience of Hebrews to the sufferings Christians might face today. To what extent are they similar and different?
- Read Hebrews 12:5. What are the two mistakes that Christians can make when life gets difficult?

  If you are in a group, have the members discuss which of these two negative responses to trials they are most susceptible to and why. In what ways is God's treatment of His children similar to earthly parenting, and in what ways does it differ?
- What was presented as the ultimate purpose of our earthly sufferings? How does this affect the way you think about suffering?

  If you are in a group, have the members discuss the following questions: Since suffering can conform us to the image of Christ, should we actively pursue suffering? Does a biblical view of suffering mean that we should not seek to alleviate our suffering or the suffering of others? Why or why not?

PRAYER

Commit what you have learned from God's Word in this lesson to prayer.

- Praise God that He is sovereign over all of your circumstances.
- Confess any doubts or questions you've entertained about God's goodness and love on account of any hardships and trials.
- Thank God for His promise that you will one day be free from all sin and suffering.
- Ask God for joy in your suffering in the reminder that you are being conformed to the image of Christ.

REVIEW QUIZ

Use these multiple-choice questions to measure what you learned from this lesson.

1. Which of the following does God most desire for His children while on earth?
   a. Health
   b. Wealth
   c. Holiness
   d. Happiness

2. The New Testament's teaching on suffering is often connected to which of the following?
   a. Joy
   b. Grief
   c. Affluence
   d. Vengeance

3. The analogy of the Olympic weightlifter relates to which of the following concepts connected to suffering?
   a. Power
   b. Victory
   c. Endurance
   d. Competition

4. What did Dr. Ferguson say is often true of people who have never experienced suffering or privation?
   a. They are unusually successful.
   b. They lack intellectual ability.
   c. They have little character.
   d. They have few friends.

5. God seeks to alleviate our suffering as quickly as possible.
   a. True
   b. False

6. What word is the term *trained* connected to when used in Hebrews 12:11?
   a. Home
   b. School
   c. Temple
   d. Gymnasium

Answer Key—Enduring Hardships

REFLECTION & DISCUSSION QUESTIONS

Before the Video

What Do You Think?

These are personal questions. The answers should be based on your own knowledge and experience.

Scripture Reading

- What should Christians do to be able to run their race with endurance? What hope does this passage set forth regarding the end result of such endurance?

  Christian must set their eyes firmly on Jesus Christ if they are to run the race that is set before them with endurance. Jesus endured the cross for the joy that was set before Him—namely, being restored to the glory He had with the Father and being seated at His right hand. Likewise, our sufferings in this life are not in vain, for we will one day also be raised in glory and honor.

During the Video

Perspectives on Suffering

- What is the non-Christian view of suffering?

  Those who are not Christians view suffering as altogether horrible and only seek to alleviate it. However, Christians can have a different perspective on suffering. Though suffering is not good in and of itself, the gospel view of suffering is that it is productive in the Christian life and used by God to transform us into the likeness of Christ.

- What is the meaning of the word *endurance*?

  The word endurance *means "to remain underneath something." The analogy of a weightlifter bearing the load of massive weights was given to illustrate the meaning of endurance. As Christians, we have various pressures in our lives, and we must learn to be able to endure them and keep standing.*

Purposes of Suffering

- According to Dr. Ferguson, what is one of the tragedies of our modern society?

  One of the tragedies of modern society is that there no longer seems to be any interest in character. Instead, the world values its own concept of success, such that emphasis is placed on personal accomplishments, when the New Testament clearly stresses the importance of developing and having character above personal success.

- What Old Testament book does the author of Hebrews quote from when discussing the topic of discipline in Hebrews 12?

  When discussing the topic of God's discipline, the writer of Hebrews quotes from the book of Proverbs: "My son, do not despise the LORD's discipline or be weary of his reproof, for the LORD reproves him whom he loves, as a father the son in whom he delights" (3:11–12). Therefore, we see that the concept of God's disciplining His children is a theme in both the Old and the New Testaments.

After the Video

- What were some of the difficulties that the recipients of the letter to the Hebrews were facing?

  Hebrews is one of the books of the New Testament that addresses hardship, difficulty, opposition, and suffering in the Christian life because the recipients of the letter were experiencing trials of various sorts. Some had been disinherited for becoming Christians. Others likely had lost their jobs. Some had to leave their homes and families. The book of Hebrews served as a brief word of encouragement to them and as an instruction for what is necessary for enduring hardships as a Christian.

- Read Hebrews 12:5. What are the two mistakes that Christians can make when life gets difficult?

  One mistake Christians can make is to regard the discipline lightly and view it as insignificant. When it has passed, we should not merely be glad that it is over, but ask, "What was the Lord was teaching me?" A second mistake is to become discouraged by the discipline. The believer must remember that a true father will always train his children, and our heavenly Father does exactly that. The encouragement of Scripture is that "God is treating you as sons" (Heb. 12:7).

- What was presented as the ultimate purpose of our earthly sufferings? How does this affect the way you think about suffering?

  God's purpose in our sufferings is that we may share His holiness, and essentially, this means being like Jesus, His holy Son. Through hardship, we are trained to become more like Christ. Dr. Ferguson alluded to Romans 8:29 when he said, "God has had His heart set upon us from the very foundation of the world that we might be conformed to the image of His Son, our Lord Jesus Christ." The remaining question is personal and should reflect on how God's purposes in our suffering affects the way you think about suffering.

REVIEW QUIZ

Lesson 10

1. **C.**
   God is not opposed to His children's having health, wealth, or happiness in this life. None of those things is inherently bad. However, in His eternal purposes, His priority for us in this life is that we would grow in holiness.

2. **A.**
   The New Testament's teaching on suffering is often connected to joy. The two are not opposed to one another. Paul says in Romans 5:3, "We rejoice in our sufferings." This biblical view of suffering is contrary to that of the prosperity gospel.

3. **C.**
   This analogy gives a picture of what endurance looks like. As the weightlifter bears up under the pressure of incredible weight and can do so only with diligent and progressive training, so believers also train throughout their lives and grow in endurance as they bear the pressures of this life.

4. **C.**
   Dr. Ferguson said that those who have never experienced suffering or privation often have very deficient character. This can be supported by the New Testament teaching that "suffering produces endurance, and endurance produces character" (Rom. 5:3–4).

5. **B.**
   God does not seek to alleviate our suffering as quickly as possible because that would prevent us from the spiritual growth that He desires us to experience through it. We must remember that God's intended purpose for our suffering as Christians is that we would be conformed to the image of His Son.

6. **D.**
   All of these environments are places in which people are trained, but it was mentioned that the word trained *is connected to language related to the gymnasium. A gymnasium is helpful for us to picture when considering our hardships of this life. Through these hardships, our heavenly Father is training us and strengthening us that we might endure in the Christian life, constantly growing in likeness to Christ.*

11

Walking as a Christian Witness

INTRODUCTION

Christians are called to be in the world but not of the world. But how can we live in this world without compromising our faith? And how can our faith make an eternal impact on those around us and help draw them to the Lord Jesus Christ? In this lesson, Dr. Ferguson looks to the book of 1 Peter to provide principles and practical instruction on how to be a faithful witness to the Lord Jesus Christ in this world.

LEARNING GOALS

When you have finished this lesson, you should be able to:

- Identify the characteristics that make Christians stand out to non-Christians
- List and explain the two levels of the Christian's response to non-Christians

KEY IDEAS

- Written to those who lived in a pre-Christian world, the book of 1 Peter remains incredibly relevant for Christians who are living in today's post-Christian world.
- The Christian's countercultural life should naturally evoke questions from non-Christians.
- The Christian's proper response to the questions of non-Christians includes using the right words, lifestyle, and attitude to communicate our hope in Christ.

REFLECTION & DISCUSSION QUESTIONS

Before the Video

What Do You Think?

Take a moment to answer the following questions. They will prepare you for the lecture.

- What aspects of a Christian's life should cause someone to ask us about our faith?

- Before your conversion, were there any Christians who particularly influenced you toward the gospel? Who were these people, and how did their witness affect you?

Scripture Reading

Now who is there to harm you if you are zealous for what is good? But even if you should suffer for righteousness' sake, you will be blessed. Have no fear of them, nor be troubled, but in your hearts honor Christ the Lord as holy, always being prepared to make a defense to anyone who asks you for a reason for the hope that is in you; yet do it with gentleness and respect, having a good conscience, so that, when you are slandered, those who revile your good behavior in Christ may be put to shame. For it is better to suffer for doing good, if that should be God's will, than for doing evil.

—1 Peter 3:13–17

- Why is it important for Christians to maintain a good conscience when suffering for righteousness' sake?

During the Video

Answer the following questions while you watch the video. They will guide you through the lecture.

The World's Questions *0:00–12:58*

- Why is 1 Peter a significant book for the Christian church in the West?

- In what ways is the post-Christian world a hopeless world?

The Christian's Answer *12:58–23:26*

- According to 1 Peter 3:15, what two qualities must Christians display when giving an answer for their hope in Christ?

- Why do Christians not need to fear those who oppose them?

After the Video

Answer the following questions after you have finished the lecture. They will help you identify and summarize the major points.

- Peter calls us to always be prepared to make a defense to anyone who asks us for a reason for our hope. How is the conventional approach to modern evangelism different from what Peter envisions?

  If you are in a group, have the members discuss the following questions: Have you ever had a non-Christian ask you about your faith? What in particular did they notice about you, and how did you respond to them?

- Dr. Ferguson named two levels for how a Christian is to answer an inquiry from a non-Christian about his faith. What is the first level of the Christian's response?

  If you are in a group, have the members discuss the following: the best way to see if you can clearly communicate the gospel is to be able to explain it to a child. How would you explain the gospel simply, in a way that could be understood by a child or someone with no prior knowledge of the Christian faith?

- What is the second level of the Christian's response?

  If you are in a group, have the members discuss both positive examples and negative examples of how Christians are to engage with non-Christians. Practically speaking, what does gentleness and respect look like in our interactions, and what does it not look like?

PRAYER

Commit what you have learned from God's Word in this lesson to prayer.

- Praise God that He can even use suffering for His own glory.
- Confess ways in which you've failed to picture the gospel in your actions.
- Thank God for the privilege of bearing witness to others about Jesus Christ.
- Ask God that others might see your faithfulness, even while suffering, and ask you for a reason for your hope.

REVIEW QUIZ

Use these multiple-choice questions to measure what you learned from this lesson.

1. Why was the Roman Empire opposed to Christianity?
   a. Rome opposed Christianity's attitude toward Judaism.
   b. Rome opposed Christianity's multiculturalism.
   c. Rome opposed Christianity's exclusivity.
   d. Rome opposed Christianity's lack of social status.
2. Which of the following did Peter envision when he wrote his first letter?
   a. That Christians would not suffer for the faith
   b. That non-Christians would already know the gospel
   c. That Christians only needed to preach the gospel, not live it out
   d. That non-Christians would ask Christians questions about their faith
3. Which of the following is true of Christians that makes them naturally different from the world?
   a. They live in light of the future.
   b. They live in light of the present.
   c. They live in light of what is temporary.
   d. They live in light of what is visible.
4. Which of the following is *not* listed in 1 Peter 3 regarding how we are to communicate the gospel?
   a. With a good conscience
   b. With gentleness
   c. With respect
   d. With power
5. Christian families will begin to stand out more and more as family life in society at large becomes increasingly dysfunctional.
   a. True
   b. False
6. Which of the following is *not* one of the statements that surround Peter's teaching?
   a. We should be confident of the divine blessing.
   b. We should expect that we will be fruitful.
   c. We should not fear those who oppose us.
   d. We should not expect the gospel to be offensive.

Answer Key—Walking as a Christian Witness

REFLECTION & DISCUSSION QUESTIONS

Before the Video

What Do You Think?

These are personal questions. The answers should be based on your own knowledge and experience.

Scripture Reading

- Why is it important for Christians to maintain a good conscience when suffering for righteousness' sake?

  Maintaining a good conscience is important when suffering for righteousness' sake so that our good behavior in Christ might be untarnished, to the shame of those who revile us. In 1 Peter 3:18–22, Peter holds up Christ as the example of righteous suffering to support his argument, for Christ suffered and was exalted.

During the Video

The World's Questions

- Why is 1 Peter a significant book for the Christian church in the West?

  The book of 1 Peter was written to help Christians in a pre-Christian world bear witness to Jesus Christ. In the West today, we have become a post-Christian world that in many ways is similar to the pre-Christian world of the Roman Empire. As such, 1 Peter helps Christians today to navigate this world without compromising the faith.

- In what ways is the post-Christian world a hopeless world?

  Dr. Ferguson outlined the various ways the post-Christian world is hopeless. Scientists maintain that there is nothing in the substructure of life that gives life any significance. Philosophers assert that life has no meaning. People have become resigned to the idea that human life is nothing more than an accident and that we cease to exist after we die. These are a few examples that demonstrate the hopelessness of the post-Christian world.

The Christian's Answer

- According to 1 Peter 3:15, what two qualities must Christians display when giving an answer for their hope in Christ?

  As Christians, we are called to display gentleness and respect when our lifestyle—even our suffering—prompts people to ask about our hope. Gentleness means that we will display meekness and humility, taking care not to be overbearing. Being respectful involves treating all people with dignity as image bearers of God.

- Why do Christians not need to fear those who oppose them?

  "Have no fear of them, nor be troubled, but in your heart honor Christ the Lord as holy" (1 Peter 3:13). In this verse, Peter sets forth the reason why Christians need not fear any opposition: we have a greater fear for Jesus Christ as Lord. Honoring Christ as Lord in our hearts sets us free from the fear of man.

After the Video

- Peter calls us to always be prepared to make a defense to anyone who asks us for a reason for our hope. How is the conventional approach to modern evangelism different from what Peter envisions?

  The emphasis of many modern evangelistic methods tends to be on Christians' pursuing non-Christians in order to ask questions. However, when Peter wrote his letter, he envisioned that the reverse would be true: that non-Christians would be approaching Christians to ask questions. This should encourage us to be distinguishable from the world and not to approach evangelism artificially.

- Dr. Ferguson named two levels for how a Christian is to answer an inquiry from a non-Christian about his faith. What is the first level of the Christian's response?

  The Christian's first level of response is "to make a defense." This involves the testimony we express with our words about our hope in Jesus Christ, which requires telling people about who Jesus Christ is and what He has done—in other words, being able to clearly communicate the message of the gospel.

- What is the second level of the Christian's response?

  The Christian's second level of response to non-Christians consists in making a defense "with gentleness and respect." Our testimony about Jesus Christ is expressed not only in our words but in our manner, and we are called to have a lifestyle that corresponds to the word of the gospel. As Dr. Ferguson remarked, "If the gospel hasn't made a life-transforming impact upon us, the words that we speak to communicate that gospel to others will fall to the ground."

REVIEW QUIZ

Lesson 11

1. **C.**
   Christianity is an exclusive religion—only Jesus is Lord. The Romans would tolerate other religions as long as people would also confess that Caesar is Lord. Because Christians refused to make this confession, Christianity was viewed as extremist and subversive to Rome.

2. **D.**
   Peter envisioned that the lives of Christians would be in such stark contrast to the society around them that non-Christians would naturally ask them why they were so different.

3. **A.**
   Christians live in light of the future. They see beyond the horizon of this world. They understand that the present is short and eternity is long, and that the invisible world is far more real than the visible world.

4. **D.**
   Though the gospel is the power of God for salvation, the individual Christian does not need to seek to be powerful in his presentation of it. The Christian's focus, according to 1 Peter 3:15–16, is to communicate the gospel with gentleness, respect, and a good conscience.

5. **A.**
   In an increasingly dysfunctional society, people will look at Christian families and be prompted to ask what makes them so different. This will be a tremendous opportunity for Christians to share the gospel message and display it with their lives.

6. **D.**
   Christians should expect that the gospel message and the word of the cross will offend people. In fact, Scripture clearly teaches that this is the case. First Corinthians 1:18 says that the word of the cross is folly to those who are perishing, and Jesus Himself told His disciples that they would be hated by all for His name's sake (Matt. 10:22).

12

Persevering to the End

INTRODUCTION

The author of Hebrews wrote to exhort and encourage believers to continue the race of faith and remain committed to the Lord Jesus Christ amid opposition, persecution, and discouragement. In this lesson, Dr. Ferguson concludes this series by unpacking the great message of Hebrews: Whatever Christians have lost for Christ, they have given up to gain a far greater treasure in Christ.

LEARNING GOALS

When you have finished this lesson, you should be able to:

- Identify the ultimate finish line of the race of faith
- Recognize the hindrances that believers encounter while running this race
- List the three encouragements that the author of Hebrews gives to keep us running to the end

KEY IDEAS

- The Christian life is a race, but it is not a sprint. It is a marathon.
- All of the difficulties we face in the Christian life cannot compare to the joys that await us when we finish the race of faith, so we must keep our eyes fixed on Jesus.
- Though Christians are called to run their own race, they are surrounded by others who are also running and have the example of Christ who ran and finished the race before them.

REFLECTION & DISCUSSION QUESTIONS

Before the Video

What Do You Think?

Take a moment to answer the following questions. They will prepare you for the lecture.

- What is a situation that you've encountered in life that required you to persevere over a length of time? How were you able to endure it, and what was the outcome?

- Have you ever reached a point in your Christian life where you wondered if keeping the faith was really worth it? What led you to ask that question, and how did you work through it?

Scripture Reading

For the grace of God has appeared, bringing salvation for all people, training us to renounce ungodliness and worldly passions, and to live self-controlled, upright, and godly lives in the present age, waiting for our blessed hope, the appearing of the glory of our great God and Savior Jesus Christ, who gave himself for us to redeem us from all lawlessness and to purify for himself a people for his own possession who are zealous for good works.

—Titus 2:11–14

- What is connected to salvation and the appearance of the grace of God in this passage?

During the Video

Answer the following questions while you watch the video. They will guide you through the lecture.

Exhortations and Warnings to Perseverance *0:00–12:34*

- What is the finish line of the race of the Christian life?

- What is the difference between hindrances and sins?

Encouragements to Perseverance *12:34–23:16*

- What is the benefit of belonging to a church that has older members?

- What does it mean that Jesus is the "founder" of our faith?

After the Video

Answer the following questions after you have finished the lecture. They will help you identify and summarize the major points.

- What does Satan seek to do to divert believers during their race, and what must Christians do in response?

  If you are in a group, have the members discuss the following questions: When your eyes are diverted and distracted from Christ, where do you tend to focus instead, and how does this affect you spiritually?

- What three encouragements does the author of Hebrews provide Christians for the race of the Christian life?

  If you are in a group, have the members discuss the following questions: Which of these three encouragements do you find most personally helpful and why? Which of the three do you tend not to think about very much, and how might you make it a more focused part of your thought?

- At the conclusion of this study series, what is the most important thing you have learned about the Christian life? Why?

  If you are in a group, have the members discuss their answers to the above questions about the most important thing they have learned from this series and why.

PRAYER

Commit what you have learned from God's Word in this lesson to prayer.

- Praise God that at the end of the race, Jesus is waiting for you.
- Confess any specific sins that are diverting your eyes from Jesus.
- Thank God for the founder and perfecter of your faith who never stumbled, enduring suffering and temptation for your sake and for God's glory.
- Ask God to reveal to you hindrances that slow you down in your race and to grant you the power of His Spirit for the stamina to keep running it.

REVIEW QUIZ

Use these multiple-choice questions to measure what you learned from this lesson.

1. The fact that God has planned the race of each of His children was associated with which of His attributes?
   a. Love
   b. Mercy
   c. Eternality
   d. Sovereignty
2. Titus 2:11–12 relates to which of the following aspects in the Christian race?
   a. Loving others
   b. Dealing with sin
   c. Overcoming hindrances
   d. Growing in prayer
3. Which of the following is God's great concern for His children?
   a. Success
   b. Popularity
   c. Holiness
   d. Intelligence
4. Which of the following is *not* one of the three encouragements to run the race?
   a. Others surround us.
   b. God will take trials from us.
   c. Jesus has gone before us.
   d. Christ is waiting for us.
5. The doctrines of predestination and election are set before Christians in the New Testament as a threat.
   a. True
   b. False
6. Which of the following is true of the heroes of the faith in Hebrews 11?
   a. They viewed this earth as their home.
   b. They never experienced times when their faith wavered.
   c. They looked forward to the promise that Jesus would come.
   d. They received the promises before their earthly lives ended.

Answer Key—Persevering to the End

REFLECTION & DISCUSSION QUESTIONS

Before the Video

What Do You Think?

These are personal questions. The answers should be based on your own knowledge and experience.

Scripture Reading

- What is connected to salvation and the appearance of the grace of God in this passage?

  In this passage, the discipline of the Christian life is connected to salvation and the appearance of the grace of God. The Christian life is one that is characterized by the discipline of renouncing ungodliness and worldly lusts so that we might live godly lives in the hopeful expectation of the One who redeemed us for holiness.

During the Video

Exhortations and Warnings to Perseverance

- What is the finish line of the race of the Christian life?

  The finish line of the race of the Christian life is seeing the Lord Jesus Christ, the One who has been our companion in the race, in all His glory. This will occur either when Christians die and are immediately in the presence of the Lord, or when Christ returns.

- What is the difference between hindrances and sins?

  Hindrances *refers to anything in our lives that encumbers us or slows us down in the race of the Christian life. Hindrances are not necessarily sinful in and of themselves. We must be wise and discerning to know what in our lives is essential for us to glorify Christ and what is incidental, so that we are not distracted and take our eyes off of Him. Sins, on the other hand, are inherently evil, and we must always seek to deal seriously with any sins that entangle us.*

Encouragements to Perseverance

- What is the benefit of belonging to a church that has older members?

  It is beneficial to belong to a church that has older members because it gives younger Christians the opportunity to see examples of faithful living from those in later stages of life. These are Christians who have been running the race longer, and they enable younger Christians who may never have suffered significantly to witness what God in His mercy has produced through the suffering of an elderly saint.

- What does it mean that Jesus is the "founder" of our faith?

  The word founder *conveys the idea that Jesus is the One who has run the race first. He ran His race faithfully despite His suffering, and because He has finished the race, He has opened up the way for others to follow Him. As Dr. Ferguson noted, "The Lord Jesus has been clearing the jungle that our sin has created and making a way for us, so that He is the captain of our salvation. And He leads us nowhere that He has not first been Himself."*

After the Video

- What does Satan seek to do to divert believers during their race, and what must Christians do in response?

  Satan seeks to divert our eyes from Jesus. He tempts us to look inward at ourselves rather than to Christ. Further, he tempts us to look sideways at other people and compare our lives with theirs. Often, we are tempted to think that others have easier lives than we do, or that God has given them a better life. Because of this, the author of Hebrews exhorts us to keep our eyes fixed on Jesus.

- What three encouragements does the author of Hebrews provide Christians for the race of the Christian life?

  The three encouragements are (1) we are surrounded by others who have run the race, (2) Jesus has gone before us and has run the race to the end, and (3) Christ is waiting for us at the end of the race.

- At the conclusion of this study series, what is the most important thing you have learned about the Christian life? Why?

  These questions are subjective, so answers will vary. Answers should take into consideration the wide range of subjects that Dr. Ferguson covered in this series such as what it means to be a Christian, to belong to a church, to grow in grace, and to persevere to the end.

REVIEW QUIZ

Lesson 12

1. **D.**
   The fact that God has planned each of our races was associated with God's sovereignty in this lesson. The Father has planned our lives, and nothing can hinder and thwart His good plan. As we follow His revealed will in His Word, we can be confident that He knows exactly what He is doing in our lives.

2. **B.**
   Titus 2:11–12 calls believers to deny ungodly lusts. When there is sin in our lives, we should not take it lightly by reckoning that we are forgiven by God. God's grace in Jesus Christ is given to us in order to deal with sin, not so that we will tolerate sin.

3. **C.**
   God's great concern is that we be holy as He is holy. When we tolerate sin, we fall behind in the race and, eventually, fall out of the race. God's purpose in saving us is that we might be conformed to the image of His Son, who is perfect in holiness and righteousness (Rom. 8:29).

4. **B.**
   While God knows exactly how long any given trial of ours will last, and at times He does remove specific trials from our lives, this is not one of the encouragements offered in the book of Hebrews, nor is there a guarantee that trials will be removed in this life.

5. **B.**
   These doctrines are not a threat to Christians but rather are a great consolation and encouragement. Because of God's sovereignty, we can know that the Father has already planned what will happen to us in our lives, and we can rest assured that He knows exactly what He is doing, even if it is painful and we do not understand the reasons from an earthly perspective.

6. **C.**
   The individuals in Hebrews 11 all lived by faith. They believed in God's promise that He would one day send the Messiah, even though they didn't see Jesus come during their earthly lives. As we run our Christian race, we can think of this great cloud of witnesses watching us and cheering us on, and as we think of the example of their lives, we can be encouraged.